MANLY DOMINION

MANLY DOMINION

in a passive-purple-four-ball world

mark chanski

CALVARY PRESS PUBLISHING
MERRICK, NEW YORK
www.calvarypress.com

CP Calvary Press Publishing
2005 Merrick Road, #341
Merrick, New York 11566

ISBN 1-879737-55-8

1. Christianity 2. Christian Men 3. Christian Parenting
4. Christian Marriage 5. Applied Theology

Cover and Book Design: Anthony Rotolo

Manufactured in the USA
2 3 4 5 6 7 8 9 10 06 07 08

To my Dianne,
My intelligent, beautiful, and servant-hearted Abigail who does good to me all the days of her life.

Acknowledgements

The Lord has been so gracious to give many wise counselors and helpers who have directly assisted me in the writing of this book. I can only mention a few:

Geoff Thomas whose early reading and encouragement brightened my eyes; Dr. Joel Beeke whose advice and help I've cherished; Dr. Jay Adams and Sam Waldron whose later reading and recommending paved a way; Craig Sietsema and Dave Chanski whose surgically sought opinions have been as apples of gold in settings of silver; Dianne Chanski whose mind became my most frequently consulted source; Marcie Filcik, whose stylistic recommendations have been greatly appreciated; Joseph M. Bianchi, who accepted for publication and painstakingly improved my manuscript.

Table of Contents

Introduction

On September 11, 2001, terrorism struck America. Passenger-filled, fuel-swollen commercial airliners hijacked by jihad driven fanatics impaled both World Trade Center towers. The twin giants billowed smoke and fire, then collapsed before our eyes. Another plane slammed into the Pentagon in a ball of fire. A third hijacked aircraft, apparently heading toward the U. S. Capitol Building or The White House in Washington D.C., crashed into a Pennsylvania farm field. A heroic band of passenger patriots had stormed the terrorist controlled cockpit, foiling their monument-destroying bid.

When the terrorist smoke had cleared, over three thousand of our countrymen had been slain. In a single day, the centuries-old belief that the oceans invincibly protected us from our enemies had dried up. Our previously peaceful nation was reeling with its newfound vulnerability. The terrorists and their supporters danced in the streets, and boasted in their newfound superiority. They wouldn't hesitate to do it again.

What's a Commander-in-Chief to do?

What's a head of a household to do when a rattlesnake in the family basement bites one of his children? He's heard the report that a whole nest of rattlers now roams the downstairs. Should he cordon off the basement, making it off limits to his family, hoping that during the following days, months or years the snakes will choose not to slither up the stairs and make more strikes? Or should he gird himself with suitable armor and weapons, descend the stairs, and take out the nest of threatening devils? The former would be the strategy of a passive and timid coward, the latter the tactic of a bold and subduing man.

Note the valor attached to one of King David's renowned Mighty Men:

> **2 Samuel 23:20** *Then Benaiah the son of Jehoiada, the son of a valiant man of Kabzeel, who had done mighty deeds, killed the two sons of Ariel of Moab. He also went down and killed a lion in the middle of a pit on a snowy day.*

President George W. Bush played the man. In the face of calls for restraint, peace protests, and threats of terrorist retaliation, he stepped up and did what had to be done. Before a hushed and listening world, he thundered the Bush Doctrine, declaring that all nations that harbor and enable terrorists will be held as accountable as the terrorists. He diplomatically mustered together a coalition of allies, and then quickly unleashed the American military machine on the Taliban-ruled outlaw nation of Afghanistan. Within a matter of weeks, the nest was taken out. The heads of the snakes were crushed.

In this historical drama, we have a striking case study of Manly Dominion. Instead of passively sitting back and hoping for the best, Mr. Bush aggressively stepped up and executed a bold plan of action. His behavior is worthy of our imitation.

Since the days of *The Greatest Generation* (Depression and WWII), western culture has been bathed in the putrid, lukewarm waters of relativism, liberalism, feminism, and excuse-ism. Bold convictions on issues have been demonized as bigoted. Bold actions by leaders have been maligned as macho. Bold endeavors by individuals have been suffocated by self-doubt. True, biblical, image-bearing manhood has gone into hiding.

This book is a modest attempt to rinse off and retrain us (men and women alike) to live in accordance with the scriptural commission spoken by our Almighty Maker in the beginning:

> **Genesis 1:27-28** *And God created man in His own image, in the image of God He created him; male and female He created them. And God blessed them; and God said to them, "Be fruitful and multiply, and fill the earth, and* ***subdue*** *it; and* ***rule*** *over the fish of the sea and over the birds of the sky, and over every living thing that moves on the earth.*

May the Spirit of God bring a revival of true Manly Dominion.

Chapter 1
Manly Dominion in Scriptural Perspective: Biblical Exposition

Permit me to escort you into the home of a friend of mine. Watch your step as you follow me downstairs. We're now descending a stairway into his basement, where we open a door and enter into a handsomely furnished billiard room.

I direct your attention to two items. First, notice that solid purple four-ball resting on the green tabletop. It's a billiard ball by trade. Its chief trait is *passivity*. By *passivity*, I mean that its propensity and vocation is to be *acted upon* and *pushed around*. That is, pushed around by triangular racks, pushed around by cue sticks, pushed around by fellow balls, and pushed around by bumper cushions. The purple four-ball is a *passive* object.

The second item I want you to notice is my friend, Nick. Nick is a skillful billiard player. His chief trait is *domination*. While circling the table, Nick premeditatedly designs in his head schemes for directing specific balls to destinations he has deemed desirable. Then, with the forceful thrusts of his cue stick, he aggressively imposes his plans onto the balls and tabletop. Nick is not passive, but *aggressive*.

On the tabletop of life, many of us act more like purple four-balls than like skillful billiard players. Instead of aggressively dominating and pushing around our environment and circumstances, we passively permit ourselves to be dominated and pushed around.

This *Passive-Purple Four-Ballism* is observed in family life where men often act like couch potatoes failing to husband, father, and lead. It's seen in vocational life where men often act like drones, failing to plan ahead, work hard, and drive to excellence. It's seen in church life where men are too often AWOL failing to lead, direct, and labor. It's seen in personal life where men act like weaklings failing to buck up, exercise self control, and manage priorities.

Who of us can't relate to the strong inclination to hide behind the newspaper or computer screen instead of getting up and facing head on a pressing duty such as the need to correct a teenage son talking disrespectfully to his mother, or the need to get started on drawing up a long awaited family financial budget?

Just last week, a 2:00 am rainstorm awakened me. The downpour on the roof reminded me of the downspout we had detached two days earlier in order to mow the grass near the house. I had forgotten to reattach it. I lay passively there for ten minutes trying to convince myself that the rain would stop soon, and that therefore, I didn't need to be concerned about rushing water near the foundation seeping into the basement. It wasn't until I leapt out of bed, grabbed an umbrella, sloshed barefoot through the cold rain, and reattached the downspout, that I was able to sleep again. Finally, I acted like a man!

Yes, to some degree or another, the Passive-Purple-Four-Ball Syndrome has affected us all, and this book is intended to act as good medicine for the afflicted man. In the first chapter, we'll get "back to basics" by reminding ourselves of our God-given identity and assignment as men.

Who are we? And what are we supposed to be doing here? These are pretty basic questions.

The foundational answer is given to us in Genesis 1:27-29:

> *And God created man in His own image, in the image of God He created him; male and female He created them. And God blessed them; and God said to them, "Be fruitful and multiply, and fill the earth, and subdue it; and rule over the fish of the sea and over the birds of the sky, and over every living thing that moves on the earth." Then God said, "Behold, I have given you every plant yielding seed that is on the surface of all the earth, and every tree which has fruit yielding seed; it shall be food for you;*

Here are the first words of the Maker to man whom He created in his "image." The fact that man is identified as "image" fundamentally means that man is solemnly obligated to *imitate* God. "Be like Me," God is saying, "Do what I do." Since God had just in the previous six days exercised a governing mastery over the earth, this role as image carries profound significance.

The Lord's assignment to man carries at least *three* principle elements:

1. Subjugation

We see subjugation in verse 28 where the Lord directs man to *subdue* the earth. The Hebrew word here is *kabash*, which means *bring into bondage*, or *by force make it to serve you*. A related Hebrew word, *kebesh*, means footstool. It's used in Psalm 110:1:

> "Sit at My right hand, until I make Thine enemies a footstool for Thy feet."

Kebesh is also used in Joshua 10:24 where Joshua so subdued his enemies that he actually made *footstools* of them: "And it came about when they brought these kings out to Joshua, that Joshua called for all the men of Israel, and said to the chiefs of the men of war who had gone with him, 'Come near, put your feet on the necks of these kings.' So they came near and put their feet on their necks." Thus to *subdue* something, means to bring it into **bondage**, or by **force** make it serve you.

After Joshua's successful conquest of the land of Canaan, we read: "and the land was *subdued* before them" (18:1). Joshua and Israel had brought the formerly hostile land under their mastery.

In this way, man is to *subdue* "the earth." The planet and its functions are to be taken in hand, and brought under subjection. Man is instructed to make the earth do his bidding. He is to accomplish this by exerting forceful and aggressive effort.

Simply put, man is to be like God. God had looked on the wild plot of the earth which was "formless and void" (Genesis 1:2). He had a *plan*, and in the space of six days, God systematically and progressively put His *plan* into action. The result was an orderly world bearing witness to the genius of its Designer. And so, every image-bearing man is obligated to imitate his Maker in his own miniature world. Each man is assigned a life-long plot of wild earth that he is to stake out, cut down, plow up, plant, and harvest. "Then the LORD God took the man and put him into the Garden of Eden to cultivate it and keep it"(Genesis 2:15). We must aggressively *subdue*, and not passively *loiter*.

Every week of my life I am to reflect my Heavenly Father. Six days I labor to subdue the earth, and on the seventh day I rest, reflecting on the work the Lord has enabled my hands to do. The completed projects act as a satisfying and comfortable footstool for my feet.

2. Dominion

We see dominion in verse 28 where the Lord orders man to *rule* over the inferior creatures: "and rule over the fish of the sea and over the birds of the sky, and over every living thing that moves on the earth." The Hebrew word for rule is *radah*: to *govern, reign, hold sway over, and dominate*. God directs man to exercise lordship over all three realms of the earth: sea, sky, and ground. Furthermore, every creature within each realm: fish, birds, and beasts, is to be governed by man's will.

In Psalm 8:4-8, David celebrates man's high rank and lordship assigned to him at creation:

> *What is man, that Thou dost take thought of him?*
> *And the son of man, that Thou dost care for him?*
> *Yet Thou hast made him a little lower than God,*
> *And dost crown him with glory and majesty?*
> *Thou dost make him to rule over the works of Thy hands;*
> *Thou hast put all things under his feet,*
> *All sheep and oxen,*
> *And also the beasts of the field,*
> *The birds of the heavens, and the fish of the sea,*
> *Whatever passes through the paths of the seas.*

Man is the true "King of the Beasts," or more properly, "King *over* the Beasts." Man has been deputized by God to assert himself as ruler over the activities and inhabitants of this terrestrial ball on which he lives. So, contrary to the environmentalists who depict man as a meddling intruder on the earth, the Bible identifies man as its rightful ruler.

Man spies a wild stallion galloping across the prairie. He observes in this strong and swift beast certain abilities that will aid in transportation, warfare, and planting. So man devises a *plan* to capture the beast, fashions a harness to restrain the beast, develops a method to train the beast; and enjoys the fruit of the beast's servanthood. This entire endeavor, though horrible in the eyes of the animal rights activist, is wonderful in the eyes of God! Man is glorifying his Maker by imaging God's ruling character.

Man spies a falcon up in the sky. He observes in this high flyer a great potential aid in hunting for food and clothing. So man schemes to net the bird, train the bird, and therefore hunt with the bird. This exercise of aggressive and creative *dominion* glorifies God.

Man spies a colossal Killer Whale leaping in and out of the sea. He observes in this sea giant a magnificent spectacle for human eyes. So man contrives a method to capture the whale, transport the whale, build a pool home for the whale, train the whale, and amaze spectators' eyes with the whale. Now millions who never would have seen this masterpiece of God's hands are filled with wonder at the leaping and splashing of this amazing creature. Yes, when man responsibly exercises *dominion*, his blessed Maker is glorified.

To sum up this theme of *dominion*: God has bestowed on man both supremacy and a mandate, both an authority and an assignment. Man is God's deputy and representative on the earth. Therefore, man is obligated to exercise an assertive, aggressive and goodly rule over the various realms of God's creation.

3. Possession

We see *possession* in verse 29 where the Lord says, "Behold, *I have given you* every plant yielding seed that is on the surface of all the earth, and every tree which has fruit yielding seed; it shall be food for you." God here extends to man ownership and proprietorship over the vegetation of the earth. The Lord has signed the real estate deed, and handed it over to man in order that he might satisfy his appetites and needs through wise stewardship. Man has a God-given right and obligation to consume the products of the earth that he might be comfortably sustained.

Man spies a beautiful forest full of prime fir trees. He observes in this vegetation a valuable source of building material for homes, boats, and paper products. So man devises a method for clear-cutting the forest, and if he deems it geographically fitting, replants it with small saplings that his sons might reap a like harvest in decades to come. On the other hand, man may assess the area better suited for a shopping mall, where his fellow men that live in the area might find easier access to groceries, clothing, and lumber.

The environmentalists have it upside down. They've placed man under the feet of his environment. The Bible tells us right side up. God has placed our environment under our feet. It has been given to man as a possession. When we stroll through and manage our forests, we are not interfering trespassers, but rightful owners and stewards. We've been assigned by God to subdue them, rule over them, and use them for *good*.

I underscore that word "good." Godly stewardship over the creation requires that we subdue and rule not recklessly, but nobly, with a *good* end in view. We're to imitate the example of the blessed Maker who designated his six-day wonderland masterpiece as *very good*. We dare not thoughtlessly *vandalize* his workmanship. Rather, we're to wisely cultivate it, rearrange it, and develop it in such a way that it lovingly nurtures our fellow man (Matthew 22:39), kindly regards created beasts (Proverbs 12:10), and tastefully highlights our Heavenly Father's glory (Psalm 19:1; 104:24). This exciting errand calls for prayerful reflection.

Conclusion

One predominant principle rises out of our biblical exposition. Man is to aggressively *dominate* his environment, instead of allowing his environment to *dominate* him. I am not to be a passive-purple four-ball! I am rather to be a stick-carrying player! In the spheres of my life, I must *subdue* and *rule*, and not permit myself to be subdued and ruled. We have been commissioned by God to go out and aggressively assert ourselves as masters over every realm of our lives. I have not been assigned to stare out my bedroom, living room, or office window, passively daydreaming about what I *might* do, *if only* there weren't so many obstacles. Rather I am to get out there, so help me God, and plan it, clear it, and *do it*, with all my might, to the glory of God.

> **Ecclesiastes 9:10** *Whatever your hand finds to do, verily, do it with all your might; for there is no activity or planning or wisdom in Sheol where you are going.*

Life is short. Opportunities are many. What we do, we must do aggressively and quickly.

Chapter 2
Sinful Misconceptions: The Victimization Mindset

I recently saw a flag traditionally carried by a particular Army unit. Its slogan read:

I can and I will.

In contrast, many of us carry around an invisible flag that reads:

I probably can't, so I won't even try.

Such a cowardly mindset flies in the face of the perspective we saw in the first chapter. The biblical perspective on life is inspiring, emboldening, and liberating. Adam was created in the Garden of Eden to *subdue* and *rule*. But in reality, we're no longer in Eden. In this fallen world, sin and the curse have produced a perverting influence that strives to turn things upside down, to put man under creation's feet. In the Garden, the serpent lobbied for the adoption of his perverted worldview by *casting doubt* on God's established order with the question:

> "*Indeed, has God said . . . ?*" (Genesis 3:1)

Adam and Eve bought Satan's seductive lie, and exchanged their liberty for chains.

Many of us individually, and our modern society generally, have bought a false bill of goods regarding our worldview. Instead of believing and obeying the Lord by living with an aggressive *Dominion Mindset*, we've adopted and disobeyed Him by living with a passive

Victimization Mindset. When confronting an intimidating challenge, we've enabled each other to habitually say, "I'm helpless. I can't."

"*I can't* gain mastery or confidently assert myself in accomplishing this difficult task *because I'm a victim* who suffers from certain disqualifying handicaps. Therefore, I'm neither able nor obligated to even try. So instead of *going out* and *doing it*, I'll just *sit back* and *make excuses*."

Consider the following *Four-Ballisms*:

Four-Ballism #1: "I'm a Genetic Victim"

"I wish I could obey God and exercise dominion over my out-of-control life, but I'm shackled by what my grandparents did to me. *They've* handcuffed me!"

"What do you mean, *they've* handcuffed you?"

"They gave me these genes that I carry around with me every day. You know, my genetic disposition, my DNA and my chromosomes. Therein lies the source of my troubles."

With this kind of reasoning, one blames his hot-tempered personality on his German bloodlines. "That's why I lose it so often. It's really out of my control."

And another blames his drunkenness on his *chemical makeup*. "It's not your fault," says the alcoholic's counselor, "you inherited bad body chemistry from your forefathers." So the alcoholic goes home and reports to his wife and children that he's not sinning; he's just sick.

The media propaganda machine pushed hard to make us believe that a former President's sexual indiscretions were the result of a newly hatched disease called a "sexual disorder syndrome" commonly found in high achieving "Type A" personalities endowed with a high level of testosterone! How could we blame the poor guy? In fact, it's been craftily suggested that we need to sympathize with a lot of poor guys around the country suffering from the same infirmity.

Another parent claims that his high-energy child can't control himself or concentrate in school because he has ADD (Attention Deficit Disorder). "The psychologist says that his disobedience has nothing to do with the amount of discipline I now give to him, but rather with the kind of genes and chromosomes I long ago gave to him." The boy is simply not responsible for his behavior. He's a genetic victim.

In our culture, obese people often claim that their grossly overweight condition is not due to a lack of self-control, but to a fat-producing metabolism.

A homemaker claims that her home is in a shambles because she's just not mentally wired to be a "multi-tasker." Though Ecclesiastes 10:18 says, "*Through indolence the rafters sag, and through slackness the house leaks*," she claims it has nothing to do with sinful laziness, only with genetic predisposition.

In these ways and many more, modern man exempts himself from his God-ordained *dominion* mandate. We unashamedly develop complex *excuses* for not exercising dominion in the various spheres of our lives. Instead of *aggressively* striving to dominate our environment, we *passively* permit our environment to dominate us.

Such up-side-down perversions of God's created order are ugly to the eye. Imagine the ugly sight of a pit-bull dog terrorizing a child cornered in the backyard. We rightly object: "God didn't intend beasts to treat man that way! Beasts aren't to subdue man!"

Now think back on the ugly sight of that two-year old, tantrum-throwing boy terrorizing his mother in the supermarket aisle. We should also protest: "God didn't intend that children would terrorize and subdue their parents under their feet!" But instead, we justify the acceptability of such up-side-down ugliness with the all-too-common plea of *genetic victimization*. It's not the child's or the parent's fault. It's the high testosterone levels in the boy.

Four-Ballism #2: "I'm an Emotional Victim"

"My problem is not my genetic make up. My problem is my upbringing. You know, the way that my parents and significant others treated me in my early years."

"What do you mean?"

"It's like wet cement. When I was young and soft, the people around me made certain impressions on my emotional make-up. Now I have to live with the reckless indentations they made on my psyche."

One man claims that his Dad always said, "You'll never amount to anything." That's why he couldn't finish high school. Another painfully remembers that his Dad would at times irritably ask him, "What's the matter with you?" He traces his inability to handle stress in the workplace to this *emotional language abuse*. "I'm a victim."

Brice sadly recounts how at the tender age of eleven, his playboy Dad up and left the family fatherless. This, he claims, is why he can't now overcome his insecurities and stand up to take leadership in his own home amidst his wife and his children.

Marcia traces her present obesity back to the summer afternoon during her early teen years when her uncle took her behind the barn and abused her by sexual fondling. "Because of what he did to me, I just can't control how much I eat. I use my extra pounds as a defense mechanism. Food makes me feel secure. I'm a victim, and that's why I can't get mastery over this area of my life."

Since Tom has been back from Iraq, he hasn't been able to hold down a job for more than nine months. "Hey," says Tom, "If you'd have seen the things that I've seen over there, you'd be pretty messed up too." He's convinced he's a permanently handicapped victim.

For like reasons and countless more, we often justify the feeling that we can't succeed, and excuse ourselves from habits we should establish. That's why we can't aggressively get out there and find a job. That's why we can't succeed in school, keep the house clean, stay off drugs, get up on time, keep our commitments, and do our devotions. That's why we're not responsible to *subdue* and *rule.*

Please understand that I'm not unsympathetic to the painful scars left behind by sinful abuses done to dear souls by ignorant and evil people. I ache and grieve about such abuses. We need to *weep with those who weep* (Romans 12:15).

However, I don't believe that I'm being a true friend to people by encouraging them, in the name of sympathy, to abdicate their duties toward God. Simply being a victim determines nothing. Millions of verbally abused children grow up to be successful students, businessmen, and pastors. Thousands of fatherless boys have become outstanding heads of households. Countless sexually abused teen girls have grown to be well adjusted and physically fit women. Innumerable war veterans have returned home to become mighty pillars in our nation, despite viewing unspeakable carnage.

Again, simply being a victim determines nothing. Victims have the solemn obligation to respond to their abuse in a God-honoring way. The call away from the excuse making of *victimology* is not cruel, but very kind and liberating!

What a blessing it is to know that by the grace of God, I can break these shackles, stand up on my own two feet, and *subdue* this sphere of my life to the glory of God!

Four-Ballism #3: "I'm a Circumstantial Victim"

"My biggest problems aren't my genetic makeup or my emotional scars, but rather my *supporting cast.* It's my *present environment* that sabotages my every attempt to get my life in order. My life is swarming with *antagonists* that make my life impossible. That's why I can't *subdue* and get the upper hand on my out-of-control responsibilities and duties."

Trevor claims that he's not been able to hold down a job because of the run of obnoxious supervisors he's had to deal with at his last three places of employment. He pleads that they were all power hungry egotists who refused to take any of his advice. That's why his family is in a financial mess.

Randy blames the sharp-tongued argumentativeness of his wife for his habitual retreating down to the basement computer room where he spends hours on the Internet instead of upstairs in the living room parenting his sons and managing his household. "I'm the victim of a contentious woman."

Amanda traces her ever-present piles of wash in the laundry room, and piles of dishes in the sink, back to the insensitivity of her husband. "He's always criticizing my housekeeping. It seems like he's never satisfied. He hardly ever tells me that I'm doing a great job, hardly ever encourages me. In this non-affirming climate, I'm just not motivated to enthusiastically dive into my tasks." She also mentions that her high-energy two-year old son is to blame for siphoning off crucial time and energy.

When explaining why he's not been reading his Bible and praying for the last six months, Jonathan cites the impossible demands that his company places on his daily schedule. "If I don't arrive at the office very early, and work at home through my full briefcase late into the night, I won't be recognized as a company man. And that doesn't leave much time for personal devotions."

We all find it very easy to blame our present circumstances for our inability to responsibly *get a grip* that we might *subdue* and *rule*. We all too frequently find the excuse-making violin under our chins. "I don't do what I'm supposed to do because I'm a helpless *victim of my circumstances*."

That's why I'm a passive-purple four-ball. I'm a genetic victim. I'm an emotional victim. I'm a circumstantial victim. That's why instead of *aggressively* dominating my environment, I *passively* permit my environment to dominate me.

Again, instead of believing and obeying the Lord by living with an aggressive *Dominion Mindset*, we too often cop out and disobey Him by living with a passive *Victimization Mindset.* When confronting an intimidating challenge, we've enabled each other to habitually say, "*I'm helpless; I can't.*"

"I can't gain mastery or confidently assert myself in accomplishing this difficult task because I'm a victim who suffers from certain disqualifying handicaps. Therefore, I am neither able nor obligated to even try. So instead of going out and doing it, I'll just sit back and make excuses."

Chapter 3
Old Testament Illustrations

One afternoon, my seven year-old son, Nathan, came home from school a bit disappointed. His teacher had announced that the second graders would no longer be able to play soccer at recess or lunch hour. Work equipment for a school construction project would be parked in their section of the playground for the remainder of the school year. They'd have to be content with monkey bars and swings! Nathan wasn't happy. Neither was his Dad.

When I asked him what he was going to do about it, he said that there was nothing he could do. "I'm just a kid, Dad!"

"Maybe if you wrote a letter to the principal, Mr. Kuiper, he'd find a place for you to play soccer."

With a doubtful pencil, Nathan wrote an interesting series of imperfect sentences, entreating his principal to make an executive order on behalf of the second grade soccer enthusiasts. The next day, he shyly dropped off the crumpled envelope in the school office. By late afternoon, Mr. Kuiper appeared at the classroom door asking for Nathan. He handed to him a formal letter on official stationary. It described how Mr. Kuiper had discussed the matter with the construction crew and the teachers. A suitable soccer field had been created especially for the second graders! Nathan was amazed.

Nathan didn't curl up into a passive four-ball. Though filled with all kinds of self-doubt, he took in his hand the stick available to him, and with the help of God, he went out and *did it*. He tried, subdued, and actually changed the world!

Let's consider some saints *who just did it*.

The Bible is full of godly souls who, when confronted with daunting tasks, took seriously their dominion mandate. We'll notice that in each case, plenty of *excuses* were readily at hand. But they didn't say, "I can't!" Instead, by grace, they resolved, "I can, so help me God!" We do well to imitate their faith.

Noah

In Genesis 6: 14-15, Noah was confronted with one of history's most intimidating errands.

> *Make for yourself an ark of gopher wood; . . . And this is how you shall make it: the length of the ark three hundred cubits, its breadth fifty cubits, and its height thirty cubits.*

Understand that a cubit is approximately 1.5 feet. This translates into a multi-roomed, triple-decked sea vessel that was to be 45 feet high, 75 feet wide, and 450 feet long. That's a football field and a half in length! Also, consider the primitive tools that were going to be used to construct such a vessel.

Now, if anybody ever had seemingly legitimate excuses for curling up into a purple four-ball, Noah did. Since of all the earth's inhabitants, Noah alone found favor in the eyes of the Lord (6:8), certainly he could have pled that the sinful upbringing by his ungodly parents inadequately prepared him for such a demanding assignment. Furthermore, the bad habits of his wicked brothers probably rubbed off on Noah. Think also of his bad environment. He would be forced to build in the face of *non-affirming* worldlings who would laugh and mock at his every swing of the hammer. Finally, he had a 500 year-old body to deal with!

If anyone had a whole legion of four-ball excuses, it was Noah. But after the Lord piled on the added chores of bringing two of every living thing into the ark, Genesis 6:22 reads:

> *Thus Noah did; according to all that God had commanded him, so he did.*

Isn't this an inspiring account? There you are, a father of three little boys, standing in the middle of their cluttered bedroom on a Saturday morning. Providence has assigned you the daunting task of dry walling and painting the room. You're overwhelmed. "It's going to take me an hour just to get the beds out of here. What about the toys and clothes? This is a multi-day project. Must I move the beds back in every night? My wife doesn't want the kids sleeping in the living room. Look at them now, climbing all over the sheet-rock boards . . ."

Though you feel like exploding in anger, or hiding the rest of the day in the basement in front of a TV football game, think of Noah. God assigned him a task, and "*Thus Noah did*!" With the help of God, you can *do it* too! Don't permit yourself to be pushed around by your environment. Instead, get up and push your environment around! *Do it* just like Noah did—one board at a time.

Abraham

In Genesis 14, Abraham is faced with a pretty daunting set of circumstances. A fugitive reports to Abraham that a four-king confederacy led by the tyrant Chedorlaomer of Elam has swept down into the Jordan valley taking captive the inhabitants of Sodom, including Abraham's nephew, Lot (14:9-13). Duty is summoning Abraham to do something to rescue his blood relative; but no doubt a sense of inadequacy is haunting his mind.

The excuses may begin to arise: "I'm just an alien in a foreign land. *Who am I* to stand up to a confederacy of four kings?"

But instead of sitting back as a helpless victim under the shade of the Oaks of Mamre, Abraham snatches his cue stick into his hand and takes action. He musters his household laborers, knits together an ad hoc alliance with his Amorite neighbors Mamre, Eshcol, and Aner, and heads northward in hot pursuit of the villains. His aggressive campaign to righteously *subdue* and *rule* in this situation is crowned with success by the hand of God in Genesis 14: 15-16:

> *And he divided his forces against them by night, he and his servants, and defeated them, and pursued them as far as Hobah, which is north of Damascus. And he brought back all the goods, and also brought back his relative Lot with his possessions, and also the women, and the people.*

Abraham girded himself like a man; a man made in the image of God. So should we. When we hear a report that one of our children has been swept away into a course of folly, instead of curling up into a purple four-ball of despair, or throwing a temper tantrum, we've got to prayerfully grab the available cue stick, strategize a practical plan, and aggressively seek to break up the mess, so help us God.

Joseph

In Genesis 37, Joseph at age seventeen was brutally victimized. While obediently on an errand for his father, his envious ten half-brothers seized him and threw him into a deep wilderness pit. They then stripped him of his coat of many colors, sold him into slavery to a caravan of Ishmaelites, who re-sold him as a household servant to an Egyptian named Potiphar (37:12-36). Put yourself in Joseph's sandals. A few weeks ago, you were the heir of a wealthy Canaanite herdsman. Now, due to an abusive travesty of justice, you're believed to be dead by your father, and are carrying water for an Egyptian government bureaucrat.

If ever there was a circumstantial victim, it was Joseph. But what did he do? Did he curl up into a *self-pity ball* and brood over his misfortunes? Apparently not. He played the *bad* hand dealt to him by God's providence the best he could. With the help of the Lord, his daily diligence in the mundane household chores paid off. The impressed Potiphar appointed Joseph as chief steward over the entire wealthy household (39:1-6). Instead of moping and pouting, Joseph *subdued* and *ruled*, and the Lord crowned his aggressive efforts with success.

But you know that the story doesn't end there. Joseph is brutally victimized again. Mrs. Potiphar wickedly tries to seduce him. Joseph wisely flees from the sexual temptation, but finds himself behind bars on trumped up charges of sexual misconduct (39:7-20). Again, the imprisoned victim refuses to curl up, but takes up his jail broom, and by the Lord's kindness finds favor in the eyes of the chief jailer, who entrusts oversight of the whole penitentiary into Joseph's hands (39:21-23). Joseph sought to *dominate* his environment instead of letting his environment *dominate* him.

Apparently his big break came when the cupbearer was restored to Pharaoh's side after Joseph had favorably interpreted a dream. Genesis 40:23 says:

> *Yet the chief cupbearer did not remember Joseph, but forgot him.*

For two more years, Joseph faithfully *subdued* and *ruled* in his jailhouse plot of ground, until he was finally raised up to be the Prime Minister of Egypt (41:1-45). After thirteen years of irksome *victimization*, the Lord finally crowned Joseph's diligent head with sterling success. He actually *subdued* all of Egypt *under his feet.*

> **Genesis 41:41-43** *And Pharaoh said to Joseph, "See I have set you over all the land of Egypt." Then Pharaoh took off his signet ring from his hand, and put it on Joseph's hand, and clothed him in garments of fine linen, and put the gold necklace around his neck. And he had him ride in his second chariot; and they proclaimed before him, "Bow the knee!" And he set him over all the land of Egypt.*

Doesn't this narrative give you a surge of inspiration? You too may have legitimate claims that you are an abused victim. Your father abused you. Your uncle abused you. Your coach abused you. Your spouse abuses you. Your boss abuses you. Maybe this has gone on for years. But does any of this justify a passive, "I can't do it" approach to the challenges of life? No!

The January 12, 2002 *World Magazine* "QUOTABLES" section read this way:

> *I kept praying, trying to be strong, realizing I might get an opportunity. And the Lord gave me that.*
> —University of Texas quarterback Major Applewhite. Applewhite led his team to four touchdowns in the last twelve minutes of the Holiday Bowl game to turn a huge deficit into a 47-43 victory. The senior, Big 12 Conference offensive player of the year two seasons ago, was benched this season in favor of a stronger-armed junior, but showed exemplary character in helping and praising his competitor, and then made the most of the bowl game opportunity.

A godly Christian man who had become evidently accomplished in his vocation, in his family, and in his church, confided in me one Lord's Day evening after the worship service. He told me that in his youth he had been sexually abused. He said that this experience was emotionally and psychologically devastating in many ways. He'd been brutally victimized. He was tempted to use this nightmare part of his life as an *excuse* for imbibing in many sinful behavioral patterns for the remainder of his life. But by the grace of God, he realized that this tragedy was a *past event* that he could not permit to *bully* the rest of his life. So, "forgetting what lies behind, and reaching forward to what lies ahead" (Phil. 3:13), he courageously pressed forward to do daily what the Lord required of him as a man. The hand of the Lord crowned him with handsome success. His worst fears and insecurities were wonderfully *subdued* under his feet.

Gideon

In Judges 6, we behold a pitiable scene. The Israelites had been given the Promised Land as a possession from the Lord; but instead of subduing the land by conquering the Canaanites under their feet, they were now cowering for fear amidst the mountain dens and caves in the land (6:1-2). Because of Israel's sin, the Lord permitted the Midianites to run roughshod over His trembling people. This is what sinful patterns and a bad conscience do to a man. Instead of *boldly subduing* his obstacles, he ends up *fearfully cowering* in hiding places.

Gideon was one of those cowering Israelites. The eleventh verse of that chapter reads:

> *The angel of the Lord came and sat under the oak that was in Ophrah, which belonged to Joash the Abiezrite as his son Gideon was beating out wheat in the wine press in order to save it from the Midianites.*

Grain was supposed to be beaten out on an open threshing floor so the wind could carry away the chaff, but Gideon was cringing for fear of the Midianites in a low-lying winepress.

Such a pitiable sight may have both disappointed and amused the angel. Hadn't the Lord promised the Israelites?

> **Leviticus 26:6-8** *I shall grant you peace in the land so that you may lie down with no one making you tremble. . . But you will chase your enemies and they will fall before you by the sword; five of you will chase a hundred, and a hundred of you will chase ten thousand, and your enemies will fall before you by the sword.*

So the angel tells it like it is to Gideon:

> **Judges 6:12** *And the angel of the LORD appeared to him and said to him, "The LORD is with you, O valiant warrior.*

Twenty-first century men hide in winepresses too. After a providentially overwhelming, or conscience-smiting day, Joe returns home to hear his wife express concern about family and household issues he needs to "get a grip on." Though physically listening, he mentally slips deep down into a winepress, in which he hides to avoid facing his challenging domestic duties. Though she's talking, Joe's blocking her out. He's *wimping out.*

But we, Christian men, like Joe, need to hear the word of the Lord to us: "The Lord is with you, *O valiant warrior*." I know that at such times, we don't feel like *valiant warriors*. That's because we're looking at things upside down. These encircling duties shouldn't bring us down. We should make them our footstools. In Christ, we ***are*** valiant warriors.

> **Philippians 4:13** *I can do all things through Him who strengthens me.*

Like Gideon, we can climb up out of our mental and emotional winepresses, and put our Midianites to flight.

Just like us, Gideon was full of excuses:

> **Judges 6:13, 15** *If the Lord is with us, why has all this happened to us?... Behold, my family is the least in Manassseh, and I am the youngest in my father's house.*

But with the help of God, he and his three hundred water lapping friends were able to *subdue* his enemies, though they were *as many as the locusts in the field and the sand on the seashore*. Like Gideon, we can view ourselves as the *valiant Christian warriors* God intended us to be. We can climb up out of our depressions, and one by one attack our circumstantial opponents.

Ruth

In the Book of Ruth, we're introduced to a courageous woman who resolved to exercise holy dominion in her assigned sphere of life.

> **Ruth 1:22** *So Naomi returned, and with her Ruth the Moabitess, her daughter-in-law, who returned from the land of Moab. And they came to Bethlehem at the beginning of the barley harvest.*

Here is this Ruth the Moabitess, a Gentile social outcast in the Israelite town of Bethlehem. No ethnic group in world history was more *exclusive* than the ancient Jewish nation. To add insult to injury, Ruth was *a widow* in this foreign land. Now, left to her fears and insecurities, surely she would have curled up into a ball of self-pity and barely eked out a miserable existence for herself and her mother-in-law. But that's not how the story reads.

Instead, Ruth aggressively pursues a respectable income by

gleaning the grain left behind by the harvesters, "Please let me go to the field and glean among the ears of grain after one in whose sight I may find favor." She clearly saw her duty, and stepped forward trusting in her newfound Lord ("Your people shall be my people, and your God, my God"-1:16b), to establish the work of her hands. The Lord crowned her bold efforts with success by her *chance meeting* ("she happened to come to the portion of the field belonging to Boaz"-2:3) with the godly and dignified Boaz.

In 3:3, Ruth's mother-in-law, in seeking out provision for the future, counsels Ruth to make a bold attempt at securing the wealthy and dashing Boaz as her husband:

> *Wash yourself therefore, and anoint yourself and put on your best clothes, and go down to the threshing floor...*

What does this Gentile, foreigner, widow do? Does she succumb to her feelings of *inferiority* and *insecurity*? Does she say: "No, Mother-in-law, *I can't* do that. I'm a widow. I'm a Gentile. He won't have anything to do with me"? No. She tramples these obvious fears under her feet, and boldly invites a marriage proposal. Again, the Lord crowns her aggressive efforts with great blessing. Ruth the Moabitess eventually became the great grandmother of King David (4:17-22).

We too must never let our fears make our decisions. Fear is the most strangling emotion known to man. Who of us can't think back on all the things we failed even to attempt because of unfounded but paralyzing fear? Many young men have disqualified themselves from pursuing relationships with extraordinary young women because they were afraid she might say, "Sorry, I'm not interested."

Many capable young basketball players prematurely ended their high school careers in their freshman year by refusing to even try out for the team for fear that they might be cut. What if Michael Jordan had been cowed into hanging up his sneakers after being cut from his high school junior varsity basketball team? If my third son, Austin, had been intimidated by the doctors' assessments about the severity of his spinal birth defect, he would never have acquired his black belt in Tae Kwon Do by the age of fourteen. As we survey our lives, many of us ache regarding friends we never made, classes we never took, teams we never played for, experiences we never enjoyed, and all because we were intimidated by fears that held us down under their feet.

Shakespeare poetically put it:

> Our doubts are traitors,
> and make us lose the good we oft might win
> by fearing to attempt.

Theodore Roosevelt wisely said:

> There is no disgrace in failure, only in a failure to try.[1]

Elsewhere, Roosevelt declared:

> Far better it is to dare mighty things, to win glorious triumphs, even though checkered by failure, than to take rank with those poor spirits who neither enjoy much nor suffer much because they live in the gray twilight that knows neither victory nor defeat.[2]

Solomon put it this way:

> **Proverbs 28:1** *The wicked flee when no one is pursuing but the righteous are bold as a lion.*

We must be men and women of dominion, boldly making decisions on the basis of our duty and obligation and opportunity, not on the basis of our fears and insecurities.

David's Mighty Men

In 2 Samuel 23, we're introduced to a sampling of an elite group of Israelites called David's Mighty Men. For the most part, they first caught sight of their eventual leader when he stared down a giant named Goliath in the Valley of Elah (1 Samuel 17:19f). There stood this fearless shepherd boy who was convinced that Israel was in the right, and therefore he would defend Jehovah's name and his people's land. Though David had countless excuses to hide like his countrymen, or flee while looking up the Philistine's nostrils, instead he cut down his intimidating obstacle and delivered Israel.

Courageous acts of subjugation and dominion are *contagious.* That day, when David raised up Goliath's severed head, Israel climbed out of their holes and charged the pursuing Philistines. From that day forward, David's mighty men were inspired to imitate their king.

> **2 Samuel 23:8-12** *These are the names of the mighty men whom David had: Josheb-basshebeth a Tahchemonite, chief of the captains, he was called Adino the Eznite, because of eight hundred slain by him at one time; and after him was Eleazar the son of Dodo the Ahohite, one of the three mighty men with David when they defied the Philistines who were gathered there to battle and the men of Israel had withdrawn. He arose and struck the Philistines until his hand was weary and clung to the sword, and the LORD brought about a great victory that day; and the people returned after him only to strip the slain. 11 Now after him was Shammah the son of Agee a Hararite. And the Philistines were gathered into a troop, where there was a plot of ground full of lentils, and the people fled from the Philistines. But he took his stand in the midst of the plot, defended it and struck the Philistines; and the LORD brought about a great victory.*

Surely, Josheb-basshebeth could have cried "Uncle" because of the eight hundred to one odds. But he stayed at his post, as must the husband who's been assigned to a difficult marriage.

Surely Eleazar could have retreated with the claim that his hand was weary, but he held fast to his sword, as a man of God who must continue to take down that same scar-faced Philistine of sexual temptation again and again and again, until he's able to lie down his sword in glory.

Surely, Shammah could have fled and surrendered the field of lentils to the Philistines, but he defended the plot of ground assigned to his care, as must the Christian father whose children are assaulted by an evil culture that tries to paint him as a killjoy extremist.

> **2 Samuel 23:13-16** *Then three of the thirty chief men went down and came to David in the harvest time to the cave of Adullam, while the troop of the Philistines was camping in the valley of Rephaim. And David was then in the stronghold, while the garrison of the Philistines was then in Bethlehem. And David had a craving and said, "Oh that someone would give me water to drink from the well of Bethlehem which is by the gate!" So the three mighty men broke through the camp of the Philistines, and drew water from the well of Bethlehem which was by the gate, and took it and brought it to David. Nevertheless he would not drink it, but poured it out to the LORD;*

Heedless of the danger facing them, these three mighty men marched the twelve miles from Adullam to Bethlehem, broke through the Philistine lines, drew water from the well, and carried it back to David. Why? Simply to gratify the passing wish of their king who had long ago captivated their hearts in the Valley of Elah. It was love for their king that constrained them to these heroic feats.

Christian man of God, what ought chiefly to *constrain* us to courageous feats of valor in the field of life? What should chiefly *compel* us to overcome our excuses, insecurities, passivity, and other obstacles?: Our love for our King; our greater than David! Did He not captivate our affections when we first laid eyes on him in the Bethlehem stable as a helpless infant in swaddling clothes? He came from heaven's throne into that deep valley of humiliation in order to deliver His people from the worse-than-Goliath enemy of sin. In His death on the cross and resurrection on the third day, He holds high the head of the slain dragon of death, enabling us to shout,

> **1 Corinthians 15:55** *O death, where is your victory? O death, where is your sting?*

Each of us ought daily say, "My King has delivered me from my grave enemy. *He stood as a brass pillar till the last breath was beaten out of his nostrils.* If he so served me, it is my honor and privilege this day to so serve Him. Regardless of the blood, sweat, and tears (energy, pride, and selfishness) it may cost me, I'll do my Savior's will, and seek to grant his every wish, so help me God." This is the heartthrob of a mighty man of God; it is the heartthrob of a Christian.

> **2 Corinthians 5:14** *For the love of Christ constrains us. . .*

As Isaac Watts put it in his hymn *When I Survey the Wondrous Cross*:

> Love so amazing, so divine, demands my soul, my life, my all.

A writer of old commented on the spirit of the Greater-Than-David's mighty men:

> Wherever there is a real appreciation of who Christ is, what we are, what his vast mercy to us is, and the infinite claims of his love upon heart and life, devotion to Him becomes so complete and absorbing

> that pain, loss, and possibly death among the heathen are faced with composure when they stand between the soul and advancing Christ's interest.[3]

It's ultimately the love of Christ that constrains us to act like mighty men instead of like passive-purple four-balls. It compels us to trample down our excuses, to break through imposing obstacles, to muzzle our cowardly "I can't" whimpering, and to take our stand in fulfilling the challenging daily missions assigned to us by our beloved King.

Nehemiah

In the book of Nehemiah we meet a man who holds a position of influence in the Persian Empire. His duties as cupbearer for King Artaxerxes (1:11) were to ensure the nonpoisonous nature of his employer's food. Obviously, he was a loyal confidant with whom the King entrusted his very life. He had daily access to the royal court, and was no doubt esteemed as one competent to oversee complex tasks (2:7-8). He was part of Artaxerxes' governing "cabinet"; his "inner circle" if you will.

But instead of remaining content in his secure position in the Persian palace in Susa, he was driven by his deep love for the kingdom of God to seek out a plan for the rebuilding of Jerusalem. Having fasted and prayed, he strategized a rebuilding scheme, and boldly petitioned the king. Having secured permission and building materials, and having made a more than five hundred-mile cross-country journey, Nehemiah arrives in Jerusalem.

But the plight of the holy city is far worse than Nehemiah had expected. Sanballat the Horonite, Tobiah the Ammonite, and Geshem the Arab led hostile opposition forces. His night ride through the ruins apparently exposed devastation far more extensive than he had imagined. The main gates were broken down and consumed by fire. The wreckage was so thorough that he wasn't even able to complete his intended horseback tour. While it was still dark, he returned to camp, surely his head spinning with what he had seen.

In the morning, when he addressed the local civilians, his voice was grave. "*You see the bad situation we are in, that Jerusalem is desolate and its gates are burned by fire*" (2:17a). These priests, nobles, officials, and workingmen already knew this. That's why for so many years they had been cowed into doing nothing. The rubble piles were too daunting. The opposition forces were too intimidating.

But Nehemiah wasn't finished. He wasn't a passive-purple four-ball. He wasn't prepared to permit his environment to *push him around*. Instead, *he* would do the pushing around. He would *dominate* and *subdue* his environment, so help him God.

> **Nehemiah 2:17-18** *You see the bad situation we are in, that Jerusalem is desolate and its gates burned by fire. Come, let us rebuild the wall of Jerusalem that we may no longer be a reproach. And I told them how the hand of God had been favorable to me, and also about the king's words which he had spoken to me. Then they said, 'Let us arise and build.' So they put their hands to the good work.*

Inspired by this undaunted and subjugating man, the people of Jerusalem threw themselves into the noble task.

Thomas Edison's son Charles writes about his father's Nehemiah-like refusal to be bullied by adverse circumstances:

> [One] December evening the cry of "Fire!" echoed through the plant. Spontaneous combustion had broken out in the film room. Within moments all the packing compounds, celluloid for records, film and other flammable goods had gone up with a whoosh. . . .
> When I couldn't find Father, I became concerned. Was he safe? With all his assets going up in smoke, would his spirit be broken? He was 67, no age to begin anew. Then I saw him in the plant yard, running toward me.
> "Where's Mom?" he shouted, "Go get her! Tell her to get her friends! They'll never see a fire like this again!" . . .
> At 5:30 the next morning, when the fire was barely under control, he called his employees together and announced, "We're rebuilding!"
> One man was told to lease all the machine shops in the area. Another, to obtain a wrecking crane from the Erie Railroad Company. [4]

Ah! How often does a man arrive at his early morning devotional time to find his heart broken down in a ruinous shambles? And how often does he, after a passing inspection, walk away without any serious clean-up effort because he's overwhelmed by all the work that needs to be done?

Ah! How often does a man ponder getting his checkbook, finances, debts, budget, and investment strategy in order; but when he sees his pile of bills, his or his wife's loose spending habits, and his limited income, he throws in the towel, and instead spends his evenings watching television?

The same dynamics are present when a busy mother faces a very messy house, or when an executive who's been out of town returns to the office and sees his desk piled high with responsibilities. Or, when a student stares at a mountain of term papers and exams that must be cleared by the semester's end, when a pianist is given an intimidating piece to master for an upcoming recital, when a boy is told by his father to single-handedly shovel a long and hip-deep driveway of snow; and when a young man must take on a second job to financially provide for his family, enabling his wife to stay home with the children.

In all such circumstances, excuses abound justifying our curling up into passive-purple four-balls. But by the grace of God, we must say with Nehemiah and his friends, "Let us arise and build." This is the glorious duty and privilege of men and women made in the image of God.

But realize that Nehemiah's inspiration wasn't merely *the emotion of a moment*. Much of our enthusiasm is often short-lived and unproductive. But Nehemiah and his band stuck to their resolution. Though the quality of their work was mocked by foes (4:3), though a confederacy arose to fight against them (4:8), though they had to work with a trowel in one hand and a sword in the other (4:17), though economic pressures tempted them to beg off (5:5), and though Nehemiah was hounded by death threats (6:10), they *completed the wall in fifty-two days* (6:15).

May the Lord help us to arouse the Nehemiah-like resolution, and the "I'm-not-coming-down-till-it's-done" perseverance that dwells somewhere within all of the Spirit-born sons of God.

3 / OLD TESTAMENT ILLUSTRATIONS

1 George Grant, *Carry a Big Stick* (Nashville: Cumberland House Publishers, 1996), p. 145
2 Ibid., p.145
3 C. Chapman, from *Pulpit Commentary, Vol. 4* (Peabody, MA: Hendrickson Publishers), p. 577
4 Charles Edison, "The Electric Thomas Edison," *Great Lives, Great Deeds* (Pleasantville, NY: Reader's Digest Association, 1964), pp. 200-205

Chapter 4
New Testament Illustrations

Manly dominion didn't end with the Old Testament. New Testament saints stood on the manly shoulders of their forefathers, reaching even more impressive heights of accomplishment. Though plenty of excuses were readily at hand, they didn't say, "I can't!" Instead, by God's grace, they resolved, "I can, so help me God!"
The inspiring dominion mindset of the Apostle Paul escorts us to the feet of the perfect Man, whose holy resolution to *subdue* and *rule* eclipses all others.

The Apostle Paul

In the Book of Acts, we meet another man of God who refused, by the grace of God, to say, "I can't," and instead pressed on with the dominion mindset of "I can." His name is Paul.

After his Damascus road confrontation and conversion, the Lord called Paul to the lifelong task of taking the gospel to the Gentiles (9:15). But when he opens his mouth for Christ, the Jews plot to kill him (9:24), and he's forced into a humiliating over-the-wall-in-a-basket departure from Damascus (9:25). Imagine his self doubts at this time: "Maybe I'm just not cut out for this evangelizing business!"

Paul steels himself and shows up in Jerusalem. There, the church looks on this former persecutor with suspicion and skepticism (9:26). But instead of quitting upon the immediate rejection, he presses on in faithfulness and is eventually, through Barnabas, accepted as genuine.

This *dogged tenacity* marked the entire ministry of the Apostle as he carried out the gospel errands assigned to him by his Master. In Pisidian Antioch, the resentful hearers respond to Paul's preaching by driving him out of the district (13:50). He moves on to Iconium where the embittered audience attempts to stone him (14:5). From there, he moves on to Lystra where they actually do stone him, and drag him out of the city, left for dead (14:19).

Now if ever there was a man who had a readily available excuse as to why he was giving up and abdicating his duty, it was this wounded missionary. "Look how they're treating me. Surely this is more than one man can bear!" But Acts tells us that he arose, and the very next day went off to Derbe and preached the gospel in that city (14:20-21). By the grace of God, he would not permit obstacles, obstructionists, or self-pity to deter him from carrying out his God-assigned chores.

As a pastor, I've more than once felt wrongly shunned, miserably unappreciated, verbally stoned, and emotionally left for dead. Mondays are good days for this!

"Why do I put up with this kind of treatment? I don't need this! There are other things I can do! I don't think the Lord expects anyone to have to endure this stuff! This is the thanks I get for trying to be faithful to their souls?"

Come on, Pastor, think of Paul's scars. Think of your dear Lord Jesus' cross. Uncurl yourself from that self-pity fetal position. Let's be off to Derbe.

A deacon in our church was assigned the task of securing a modest loan from the bank in order to enable us to re-shingle our building's half-century old roof. He was able to negotiate with a certain bank representative a loan with an outstanding interest rate. The banker gave many verbal and written assurances. The praying church was informed and thanked God for His generous provision. But at the last minute, the bank representative dramatically changed the rate and informed our deacon, who immediately calculated the many thousands of additional dollars this would cost the church.

Instead of acquiescing to the obstacle and the obstructionist, the deacon armed himself with the documented truth of formal correspondence, and prayerfully marched into the bank. Initially he was rebuffed with a polite, "I'm sorry, but we can't help you." But undaunted, he pressed on to speak with higher a official who also said, "I'm sorry, but we can't help you." Still undaunted, our deacon announced that he was not yet satisfied and was not leaving until he was. The truth was on his side. Well, eventually, he left the bank that day with an, "I'm sorry we treated you and your church in such a way, and will certainly stand by our word in extending to you that advantageous interest rate we'd previously promised." Like Shammah (2 Samuel

24:11-12), the mighty-man deacon took his stand in the field of lentils and, on principle, refused to surrender the ground.

Like the Apostle Paul, our deacon had a kingdom errand, and he doggedly pursued it, even though opposed and obstructed by unwholesome and unethical forces. In this project, he acted as a man of dominion in the face of opposition. We too have been assigned by our Master to carry out countless personal, familial, vocational, and ecclesiastical chores. We should refuse to be easily hindered by minor impediments.

Consider also Paul's attitude amidst opposition. He faced his obstacles, not with a resentful heart, but joyfully. There he is in that Philippian jail. His back is bloodied and striped with the blows of persecuting rods. His feet are fastened in the prison stocks. But there he is that same night singing hymns of praise to God till midnight (16:23-25). Surely, such a high-spirited and stubbornly determined example is worthy of our imitation.

> **Philippians 3:17** *Brethren, join in following my example, and observe those who walk according to the pattern you have in us.*

> **Philippians 4:9** *The things you have learned and received and heard and seen in us, practice these things;*

May the Lord help us to be like Paul; not *excuse-makers* and *complainers*, but *subduers* and *rejoicers*!

Our Lord Jesus Christ

Now we come to Mount Everest. In the Gospels, it's our privilege to meet the perfect man, our Lord Jesus Christ. In His earthly paces we behold our ideal model for manly dominion.

His Father had given to Him a solemn assignment, a holy mandate. He must save His people from their sins. He must destroy the work of the Devil. Of all whom the Father had given to Him, He must lose none. He must press on in His agonizing redemptive labors until, "It is finished."

Consider the intimidating obstacles He faced, the fierce opponents against whom He grappled, and the countless excuses available to Him, had He chosen to play the victim instead of *act like a man* (1 Cor. 16:13).

Jesus was born into an economically poor family. Luke 2:24

informs us that Joseph and Mary were unable to afford the standard lamb sacrifice for the eighth day circumcision of their newborn. Instead, according to the poverty provision of Leviticus 12:8, Mary offered a pair of turtledoves in the temple.

Jesus was born and raised under a cloud of *social scandal.* His mother was discovered to be pregnant with Him prior to her marriage; nearly resulting in his stepfather's terminating the engagement by divorce (Matthew 1:18-19). The social stigma of an illegitimate birth no doubt hounded him throughout his childhood, and even hampered his credibility in his public ministry. "*They (the Jews) said to Him, 'We were not born of fornication*'" (John 8:41).

Parents who didn't understand or comprehend the unique mental and emotional burdens carried by their special son oversaw Jesus' youth. At twelve years old in the temple, he said to his perplexed father and mother, "Why is it that you were looking for Me? Did you not know that I had to be in My Father's house?" (Luke 2:49). Further, since Joseph's name is not mentioned after this event, it is probable that Joseph died while Jesus was yet a very young man, leaving him without the support of an intimate earthly father confidant.

Jesus' public ministry was opposed by a frontal assault of Satan. While Jesus was starving in the wilderness, the devil pounced with great temptations (Matthew 4:1-10). The whole demonic world was stirred up to defy His mission. A shrieking demon in the synagogue interrupted his Sabbath teaching (Mark 1:21-26). A whole legion of demons sought to stir up trouble for Him in the country of the Gerasenes (Mark 5:6-17).

Jesus was hounded by the Pharisees' carping criticism. They called him "a gluttonous man and a drunkard" (Matthew 11:19). He was lampooned by the Sadducees' pseudo-sophisticated reasoning. They mocked his view of the resurrection with their parable of the woman with seven husbands (Matthew 22:23-28). He was from the outset of his ministry hunted by the Herodians who sought to put him to death (Mark 3:6).

Jesus' disciples were a most frustrating group of men with whom to work. They were dull of hearing and hard of heart (Mark 8:14-21: "Do you have a hardened heart? . . . Do you not yet understand?"). They were quickly provoked to wrath (Mark 9:54: "Lord do you want us to command fire to come down from heaven and consume them?"). They were prideful and jealous (Mark 9:34 ". . . they had discussed with each other which of them was the greatest."). They were fainting and sleepy when they needed to be watchful and prayerful (Mark 14:41: "Are you still sleeping and taking your rest?").

Jesus' final hours were marked by a *wholesale desertion* on the part of his dearest friends. Judas betrayed him for thirty pieces of silver. Peter denied him three times. Upon the seizing of their Master, the other ten scattered.

Jesus' cross was one of *unbearable weight.* They blindfolded and beat him in the head after the Sanhedrin's kangaroo court. They butchered his back into bloody ribbons by scourging Him at the pillar. They thrust onto his shoulders the crude and heavy crossbeam. They drove spikes into his feet and hands. They hung him as a naked public spectacle, while his enemies passed by wagging their heads in mockery saying that if he were truly the Son of God, surely he'd come down.

He could have leaped down from the cross and swept them all into hell in an instant. He could have said, "I've had enough of this!" He could have thrown in the towel. He could have quit. He could have said, "I've been pushed beyond all reasonable limits!"

But He didn't. Instead, there He hung. He hung through His Father's abandoning Him, "*My God, My God, why hast Thou forsaken Me*" (Mark 15:34). He hung there until His Father's will was accomplished, until His errand was completed, until His chore was done, until His people had been redeemed, until He said,

> **Mark 19:30** *It is finished!*

By subduing to the end,

> **1 Corinthians 15:27** *He has put all things in subjection under His feet.*

In the Lord Jesus Christ, the Christian finds his ultimate model for subduing and ruling over the opposing circumstances of our sin cursed world. In Him, we find a hand to put over our mouths when we begin to spout our rationalizations and blame-shiftings. In him we find a holy rebuke to our every excuse for not doing our biblical duty in every difficult situation. In Him, we find a sacred reprimand to our cowardly claims that "I'm a victim, so I can't."

> **1 Peter 2:21** *For you have been called for this purpose, since Christ also suffered for you, leaving you an example for you to follow in His steps,*

> **Hebrews 12:1-3** *Therefore, since we have so great a cloud of witnesses surrounding us, let us also lay aside every encumbrance, and the sin which so easily entangles us, and let us run with endurance the race that is set before us, fixing our eyes on Jesus, the author and perfecter of faith, who for the joy set before Him endured the cross, despising the shame, and has sat down at the right hand of the throne of God. For consider Him who has endured such hostility by sinners against Himself, so that you may not grow weary and lose heart.*

John Flavel, a great Puritan, writes to us regarding our solemn obligation to aggressively and courageously, not passively and cowardly, serve Christ:

> Are you staggered at your sufferings, and hard things you must endure for Christ in this world? Doth the flesh shrink back from these things, and cry, spare thyself? What is there in the world more likely to steel and fortify thy spirit with resolution and courage, than such a sight as this? Did Christ face the wrath of men, and the wrath of God too? Did he stand as a pillar of brass, with unbroken patience, and steadfast resolution, under such troubles as never met in the like height upon any mere creature, for a trifle? Ah, did He not serve me so! I will arm myself with the like mind.
>
> Dost thou idle away precious time vainly, and live unusefully to Christ in thy generation? What is more apt to convince and cure thee, than such remembrance of Christ as this? O when thou considerest thou art not thine own, thy time, thy talents are not thine own, but Christ's; . . . This will powerfully awaken a dull, sluggish, and lazy spirit. In a word, what grace is there that this remembrance of Christ cannot quicken? What sin cannot it mortify: What duty cannot it animate: O it is of singular use in all cases for the people of God.[1]

Conclusion

I trust that this parade of biblical witnesses, with our beloved Lord Jesus bringing up the rear, has captured our hearts and gotten a hook in our consciences. Daily we stand before our God-assigned duties, and are faced with the ever-present mob of intimidating obstacles. Within are those crippling insecurities, those fears of failure that love of ease, and that slothful laziness. Without are those thorns and thistles, those antagonistic personalities, those overwhelming circumstances, and those seemingly impossible odds. We're tempted to curl up into a passive-purple four-ball. But so help us God, in the face of this mob, we must not passively surrender, but aggressively seek to subdue and rule.

It's not the passive-purple four-ball, but the stick-thrusting player that will receive from our Lord the "*Well done, good and faithful servant.*" So help us God, may this be our joyful inheritance.

I emphasize the "so help us God." Subduing labor achieves its goals only by *Divine enablement.* Noah built the ark plank by plank, but it was the Lord's doing from first to last. Remember the words of Psalm 127:1-2:

> *Unless the Lord builds the house, they labor in vain who build it;*
> *Unless the Lord guards the city, the watchman keeps awake in vain.*
> *It is vain for you to rise up early, to retire late, to eat the bread of painful labors; For He gives to his beloved even in his sleep.*

> **Philippians 2:12-13** *So then, my beloved, just as you have always obeyed, not as in my presence only, but now much more in my absence, work out your salvation with fear and trembling; for it is God who is at work in you, both to will and to work for His good pleasure.*

1 *The Works of John Flavel, Vo.1* (Edinburgh: Banner of Truth Publications, 1968), p.270

Chapter 5
Manly Dominion in Vocational Laboring: Lifelong Laboring

A typical Saturday morning begins in our home with my wife Dianne seated early at the kitchen table, with a five-columned sheet of paper spread out in front of her. Here she draws up lists of household duties for each of our five children. Duties range from balling sock pairs, to washing cars, to mowing sections of the lawn, to cleaning bathrooms, to washing windows, to pulling weeds and sweeping out the garage, etc. She then "posts" the list on the kitchen counter.

One by one, the kids climb out of bed and wander into the kitchen to see what lot has been drawn for them. Occasionally, upon reading the list, or while pulling the weeds, someone will sigh and suggest (sometimes with a grumbling voice) that he deserves better treatment than this: "Look, nobody else has to do all of this stuff like we do!"

Once it slips out of their mouth and they see me within earshot, they know what I'm going to say to them: "Hey, why were we put here, anyway? To play?"

To which, they now instinctively reply, "No, Dad, we were put here to work."

They're referring to Genesis 2:15, which establishes the creation ordinance of *work*. "Then the Lord God took the man and put him into the Garden of Eden to cultivate it and keep it." Man wasn't put into the garden to "play", or to "sport", or to "be entertained", but to "work." He was assigned to cultivate and keep the garden. He was put on the earth to *labor*!

I can remember when this first dawned on me as a young man. I 'd been recently saved at the age of seventeen. Previously I had despised work. To me, work was a necessary evil. I'd work so that I could accumulate enough money to play. At the time, I'd work a ten to twelve hour shift at a local golf course pro shop. I'd store and clean the member's golf clubs, park and recharge the electric golf carts, and pluck up one by one the driving range balls. All the while I'd be thinking how I'd rather be out at the Lake Michigan beach, or out golfing myself, or swimming in the neighbor's pool. To me, work was miserable.

But then it hit me. I can still remember sourly sitting in a cart near the pro shop door, waiting for the golfers to start returning from their rounds. "Hey, this is a bad attitude. God didn't put me here to get a tan, or to hit a ball, or to swim around. He put me here to *work*, just like he put Adam here to *work*. *Work* pleases God. He wants me to *work* with a good attitude. *Work* is a good thing, not a necessary evil!" That moment's revelation brought about a dramatic change in my *work* ethic. Sure, I still struggled with laziness and leisure-loving tendencies, but now I could evaluate this conflict biblically. I actually began to enjoy *work*.

Richard Steele, in his fine book, *The Religious Tradesman*, writes in the mid 1700s about the fundamental chore that the Lord has placed on every man's daily "to do list." God has assigned every man to *labor*.

> It is the express command and appointment of God. Adam, before and after his fall, was placed in a state of action. In innocency, the wisdom of God chose a calling for him: "the Lord God took the man, and put him into the garden of Eden to dress it, and to keep it." If noble birth, as one observes, a great estate, a small family, and a mind fitted for contemplation, would excuse man from *labour*; none had so fair a plea for it as he. After the fall when labor was more difficult to him and less profitable, he was enjoined, in the "sweat of his face to eat his bread, until he should return unto his dust."
>
> The command of Almighty God to all his posterity, is, that six days they should *labour* and do all their work;" In this is plainly implied, that all should fill up their time with some proper employment, from one

> season of religious rest to another. For it is obvious to remark, that the obligation to *labour* six days is expressed in as general terms, and is bound upon us by the same authority, as the religious observation of the seventh. Nor is the case changed under the gospel, by which men are commanded and exhorted, in the "name and authority of the Lord Jesus Christ, with quietness to work, and to eat their own bread." That his precepts might have greater force, he has given us his own example; for before his entrance into the ministerial office, we find him *labouring* in the carpenter's trade; and if so divine a person stooped to a laborious calling to teach us humility, diligence and industry, shall any who call Him their master, refuse to imitate Him herein? It is not indeed supposed that all should be employed in *labours* equally low and servile; but what is pleaded for is, that every one should fill up life in a manner becoming reasonable and accountable beings, and members related to society."[1]

For men in particular, going out to labor is a chief and solemn priority. After the fall, the woman was given her *child-nurturing* focus:

> **Genesis 3:16a** *I will greatly multiply your pain in childbirth, in pain you shall bring forth children.*

The man, in contrast, was given his breadwinner focus:

> **Genesis 3:17b-19a** *Cursed is the ground because of you; in toil you shall eat of it all the days of your life. Both thorns and thistles it shall grow for you; and you shall eat the plants of the field; By the sweat of your face you shall eat bread.*

Every man, therefore, must view the issue of his vocational labor as one of his life's greatest priorities.

In the upcoming chapters, we'll consider five areas, related to vocational labor, that call for the exercise of manly dominion: Career Choosing, Vocational Training, Job Hunting, Hard Working, and Financial Earning.

1 Harrisonburg, VA: Sprinkle Publications, 1989, pp.13-14

Chapter 6
Career Choosing

After one of my son's high school soccer games, I was sitting in the stadium parking lot discussing with my son his performance, when one of last year's seniors leaned into the open car window to say hello.

"Hey, Aaron," I said, "now that you've graduated, what are your plans? What are you going to do when you grow up?"

Aaron looked out over the lighted parking lot, wrinkled his face, and said, "I've got no clue. Haven't really thought that much about it." He went on to tell me that he was presently stocking shelves at a local grocery store.

In my opinion, it should never be that way!

Now, I don't mean to suggest that it's the responsibility of every high school senior to have pinned down his precise niche in corporate America. I do, however, believe that this vocational theme ought to have already occupied a priority portion of his teen thinking hours. Besides securing his inheritance in Christ, few issues are more important to a young man than this crucial question of vocational direction: *As an image bearer of God, what kind of work will I do in His garden, to glorify His Name?*

The Proverbs say much about man's responsibility to make plans:

> **Proverbs 16:3** *Commit your works to the LORD, And your* **plans** *will be established.*

> **Proverbs 20:18** *Prepare* **plans** *by consultation, And make war by wise guidance.*

> **Proverbs 21:5** *The* **plans** *of the diligent lead surely to advantage, But everyone who is hasty comes surely to poverty.*

The man with the dominion mindset makes plans for his vocational future. On the other hand, the man with the purple-four-ball mindset passively sits back, waiting to be struck by some wonderful opportunity that might happen to pass by.

"But I'm waiting on God! I don't want to get in His way!"

Though this may sound very spiritually minded, I believe it's a purple-four-ball cop out.

"But Adam waited in the Garden of Eden for God to tell him what to do. That's what I'm doing."

I agree that we're each to receive our vocational assignments from the Lord, but unlike in Eden, we're not to wait for some special direct revelation like His whisper in the night saying, "John, I want you to be an electrical engineer." Surely, the Lord still speaks to us, but now, through His inscripturated and inspired Word preserved in the Bible, joined together with His sovereign hand pointing out things in providence.

God now speaks to us in His scriptures and in His providence.

We must, therefore, direct our paths by the principles of the Scriptures.

> **2 Timothy 3:16-17** *All Scripture is inspired by God and profitable for teaching, for reproof, for correction, for training in righteousness; 17 that the man of God may be adequate, equipped for every good work.*

We must seize hold of the opportunities provided by providence.

> **Ecclesiastes 9:10** *Whatever your hand finds to do, verily, do it with all your might; for there is no activity or planning or knowledge or wisdom in Sheol where you are going.*

We're responsible, then, to become active students of both God's Scriptures and God's providence, assertively seeking out what the Lord would have us to labor at during the days of our lives. What contemporary vocations will enable me to keep my hands clean and my heart pure? With what gifts has God endowed me? What opportunities has God opened up for me? A man of dominion is a thinking man. He's a man who thinks ahead.

Contemporary pop notions of "discovering God's will" often ignore this concept of actively thinking ahead. Sinclair Ferguson, in his book *Discovering God's Will*, insightfully writes:

> At the end of the day, *we* will have to decide what the will of God is! We get very readily confused here about false ideas of the nature of God's guidance. We look for supernatural revelations, when God means us to live by his word. We want to abandon our normal thought-processes, when God wants us to bear the burden of thinking through his purposes for our lives. [1]

So, regarding the choosing of a career, we're not to depend on midnight whispers, tingly feelings, or damp fleeces on the dry ground. We're to responsibly evaluate and think ahead. We're not to permit ourselves to be passively pushed around by the billiard balls and bumpers of ambiguous circumstances, emotions, and impressions.

Let's say Charlie's nearing the end of his sophomore year at the state college. He's now sitting in the waiting room of his guidance counselor's office. It's deadline time to declare his major. He's procrastinated on this important decision. He's tossed to and fro by waves of indecisiveness. As he waits, he notices a bookshelf full of material regarding career options. Charlie reaches for a glossy-covered, red and yellow book, but down onto the ground tumbles another volume, opened and face down. Charlie bends down to pick it up and notices it just happens to be opened to the section entitled "Meteorology." He thinks to himself how he's always admired the local weatherman back home. In his groping and vacillating mindset he convinces himself that this must be a sign from the Lord. So that very afternoon Charlie announces to the guidance counselor that he's going to pursue a career in meteorology!

Or, say Larry's been procrastinating just like Charlie. He's miserable. It's deadline time and he doesn't have a clue regarding a college major or career direction. But Sunday morning, Larry's pastor makes an impassioned plea for young men to pursue the full-time Christian ministry as pastors. Directionless, Larry hears this sermon, is emotionally moved, and draws the conclusion that God is calling him to be a pastor. He's never seriously studied or wrestled through the biblical qualifications of a pastor described in 1 Timothy 3:1-7 and Titus 1:5-9. Moreover, church leaders who know him well have never encouraged him in this area. All Larry knows is that this peculiarly timed sermon has given his troubled mind a sense of peace.

I suggest to you that such scenarios are examples of a passive, irresponsible, unthinking, and dominion-abdicating approach to career choosing. They may have a veneer of spirituality about them, but are in fact unspiritual and immature. I don't mean to imply that circumstances like a book's falling open to the "Meteorology" page, or a sermon's being timely preached on the "Ministerial Call," are *irrelevant*. I simply contend that such things are not *decisive*. From the looks of it, neither Charlie nor Larry has made a career choice based on wise and prudent dominion principles.

Consider, in contrast, Jerry. Since his elementary years in school, his father frequently discussed with him his need to discover and develop his gifts so that he might serve God with all his might in his life's work. Certain passages were regularly pressed to Jerry's conscience:

> **Matthew 25:15-18** *And to one he gave five talents, to another, two, and to another, one, each according to his own ability; and he went on his journey. 16 Immediately the one who had received the five talents went and traded with them, and gained five more talents. 17 In the same manner the one who had received the two talents gained two more. 18 But he who received the one talent went away and dug in the ground, and hid his master's money.*

"Don't bury any of your abilities, Jerry! Assess what the Lord's given to you, and invest it all to his glory. Remember that the foolish servant was severely scolded not for embezzling his talent, not for riotously spending it, not for hiring an arsonist with it and burning down the Master's house, but simply for hiding it and failing to use it properly!"

> **Romans 12:6** *And since we have gifts that differ according to the grace given to us, let each exercise them accordingly:*

"So, Jerry, what gifts do you think the Lord has put into your package?"

> **Luke 12:48** *And from everyone who has been given much shall much be required.*

"Do you really think, Jerry, that this report card grade in math shows that you've been working up to your potential?"

Now, by the time Jerry has reached his senior year in high school, much of his future career has come into focus. He's recognized peculiarly strong abilities in mathematics and has accordingly pushed himself hard so that he's doing very well in Pre-Calculus class. He's performed capably in biology, chemistry, and physics. This more rigorous choice of classes has positioned him to score well on his ACT/SAT college entrance exams. His skills in mechanical drawing and computer-aided-design have opened up a part-time job opportunity with a construction firm in town. He's spent time talking with professional men in his community about career direction. He's evaluated financial income ranges, job availability forecasts, and working condition testimonies. As a result, he's made a decision to pursue an engineering degree with a mechanical/construction design emphasis. He's found a college with a high reputation in this field, and has been accepted.

I present the Jerry scenario as an example of the dominion mindset applied to career selection. Sure, it's an ideal picture. As he moves through college, his plans may be tweaked or even overhauled. The point is that *Jerry has a plan*! He's seeking to actively and purposefully chart out a course for the future. He's worked hard educationally, assessed his personal aptitudes and inclinations, researched pay scales, surveyed the field of alternatives, and sought out wise and experienced counselors.

> Fathers, seriously take up your role as counselor and guide to your sons. We've got to help our young people make plans. It was a maxim among the Jews that "he who teaches not his son a trade, teaches him to be a thief."[2]

This is an area crying out for wise fathers to apply *manly dominion.*

Finally, remember how important it is to simply make a choice. Excessive procrastination is a curse to any life. In his excellent biography of Winston Churchill, Stephen Mansfield writes about the striking trait of Churchill's decisiveness as a man of action:

> As a man of action, nothing frustrated him quite like uncertain, passive leaders...
>
> First, *they lacked the will.* Churchill knew that victory graces those whose basic attitude is action and strength rather than vacillation and meekness, that even knowing what to do is not enough without the will to do it. "It is one thing to see the forward path," he believed, "and another to be able to take it." It is a simple philosophy, perhaps, but the simplicity makes taking the first step easier: "If you travel the earth, you will find it is largely divided into two classes of people—people who say,

> 'I wonder why such and such is not done' and people who say 'Now who is going to prevent me from doing that thing?'"
>
> Second, *they lacked a plan.* Even if one possessed the will to act, it would not be enough without a plan. "*It is better to have an ambitious plan than none at all,*" he believed, and he spent large amounts of time planning in anticipation of crises while those without wise planning were overwhelmed and immobilized by events.
>
> Third, *they wanted perfection.* Without it, they would do nothing. Churchill knew that any policy or battle plan has to be fine-tuned once in progress, so he never expected perfection from the beginning. He mobilized while others micro-managed because he understood that the details could be changed later; the critical need was action. 'The maxim, "Nothing avails but perfection," he said, "may be spelled, *P-a-r-a-l-y-s-i-s.*"[3]

It's a sad sight to see a man in his late twenties who still doesn't know *what he wants to be when he grows up*! He's squandered his precious and valuable youthful years by aimlessness and indecisiveness.

> **Ecclesiastes 9:10** *Whatever your hand finds to do, verily, do it with all your might; for there is no activity or planning or knowledge or wisdom in Sheol where you are going.*

What you do, do it quickly. Life is short. Act decisively.

Playing billiards with a "shot time-limit" is quite challenging. You've got to size up the table and ball configuration quickly. Walking meditatively around the table with the cue stick in your hand isn't enough. You've got to efficiently use your time and decisively make a decision regarding your plan. Indecisive procrastination results in your time running out, and the loss of your turn.

Making no decision is the worst decision, but a decision nevertheless. On the billiard table, it's a silly mistake. On the table of life, it can be a costly tragedy.

In contrast, we ought to view ourselves as men of destiny, each created by the Lord and placed in this garden, in this world, with a very important task to accomplish.

Take Winston Churchill again. His father, Lord Randolph, perceived his young son was sickly, weak, retarded, and handicapped with a troubling speech impediment. He repeatedly told his son that he'd never amount to anything. But Winston was driven by a different conviction. He pushed himself to excel in military exercises, academic studies, and political endeavors, until he found himself the Prime Minister of the UK during World War II. So positioned, Churchill was used by God to lead his nation through its darkest hours. With his motto, "Never give in, never give in, never, never, never," he ushered Britain to its finest hour.

Mansfield, Churchill's biographer writes,

> In earlier, more Christian eras, men believed they were moved by a force that today, in our world of evolution and random chance, is taken for arrogance and license. It was the power of predestination, of God's choosing and ordaining every life for a purpose. . . Untold numbers have been moved to attempt what on their own strength, without the guarantee of a fixed destiny, they would never have begun.[4]

Mansfield argues that Divine providence was a mainspring that drove Churchill to plan and chart out a course to dare and accomplish great things. Regarding the man who believes in predestination, Mansfield asserts:

> He believes that the choices he makes merely accomplish the purposes set for his life. It makes him bold and courageous. He has confidence he will achieve his destiny and that death will not come until it is fulfilled. . . . During World War I, [Winston] wrote to [his wife] Clementine, . . . 'Over me beat unseen wings.'[5]

That's how we should view our lives. Each of us has been endowed with talents and opportunities to accomplish great things in the Lord's world. Let us each eagerly study how we can fully invest our packages to the glory of God. Let us each be driven by an Esther-like conviction that the Lord has raised us up *for a time such as this*. Let us each aggressively find something peculiarly suitable for our hands to do, and verily, do it with all of our might.

So, what's your plan? What's your child's plan? What's your grandchild's plan? Don't be a purple four-ball. Get moving, today!

1 Edinburgh: Banner of Truth Publications, 1986, p.78
2 Gardiner Spring, *Power in the Pulpit* (Edinburgh: Banner of Truth Publications, 1986), p.187
3 Stephen Mansfield, *Never Give In* (Elkton, MD: Highland Books, 1995), p.100
4 Ibid., p.106
5 Ibid., 107

Chapter 7
Vocational Training

"Alright," says the young person whose life pulses with great potential, "I think I've been given some pretty useful abilities." He's convinced he's got what it takes to become an engineer, a physician, a physical therapist, an attorney, an accountant, or a teacher. "But you know, when I think of all of that paperwork I'll have to wade through, and all of that testing I'll have to do, and all of that tuition I'll have to pay, and all of those hurdles I'll have to jump, I don't know if I have the drive to do it." Often, a natural aversion to detailed and strenuous planning, results in a fixed intimidation, that ends in the young person's de facto "passing" on higher education and training.

This "passing" on vocational training is a peculiar plague among American males; the very ones who should be the "bread-winners" (Genesis 3:17-19) in our families. During the 80's and 90's, colleges and universities witnessed a troubling demographic shift in their student bodies. Previously, young men training for professional careers filled the clear majority of classroom chairs. But now females constitute the clear majority in almost all colleges and universities. Admissions officers lament the dearth in the numbers of serious-minded male students motivated to work and study hard toward academic achievement. In some traditionally male dominated institutions, the women now outnumber the men by more than two to one.

What's the problem here? Why this epidemic of apathy and aimlessness among our young men? I believe it's another symptom of the plague of passive-purple-four-ballism that's ravaged our land.

We've got to seize the day!

A few years ago, I was studying early one morning in my basement office when my wife poked her head in and told me about how she couldn't take her usual morning walk. The neighbor's bull (that's right, horned bull) had gotten loose and was wandering the neighborhood. "I'm afraid he's going to gore me!" Sure enough, there he was, a rip-snortin' menace, pacing back and forth on the gravel road. Wanting to get back to my studies, my solution was to drive Dianne past the bull and let her walk on the section of road beyond the bovine. Surely by the time she'd return from the other direction, the bull problem would've been corralled. When our van attempted to pass him, he actually challenged our front grill! Having dropped Dianne off, a quarter of a mile down the road, my concerned five year-old Nathan said: "If I had a wife, and a bull was chasing her, I'd go and get my wife in the car and bring her home." Soundly reproved for my passive negligence, I turned the van around, gathered my (and Nathan's) treasure, and brought her home.

My manliness having been awakened, I realized I couldn't let the bull endanger other people's wives or children either. But I knew that I as a city boy was no match for the bull. The neighbor wasn't home, so I went across the street to get Mike, the beekeeper. Mike is a rustic fellow known in the neighborhood for his courage in facing aggressive beasts. His plan was for him to grab a bucket of grain from the neighbor's barn, and with it, entice the bull back through the barn door and slam it shut for the capture. All went well until the bull actually neared the barn. Instead of following the bucket of grain Mike had tossed into the barn, the bull charged—actually charged—the beekeeper! I was horrified. Mike would be gored and pinned against the barn wall. But then Mike did something extraordinary. He grabbed the bull's horns! That's right, he literally *grabbed the bull by the horns*! The effect of the beekeeper's forceful grab and jerk was striking. The seemingly fierce bull stopped in his tracks: he was stunned, intimidated, and subdued. Quickly, Mike thrust the bull toward the barn door. The beast acquiesced, and Mike slammed the door shut behind him.

On every road to vocational readiness paces many an intimidating bull. One at a time, each obstacle must be aggressively "grabbed by the horns." Extraordinary things happen in the lives of men who on principle seek to *subdue* and *rule*.

7 / VOCATIONAL TRAINING

1 Samuel 14:1-14 *Now the day came that Jonathan, the son of Saul, said to the young man who was carrying his armor, "Come and let us cross over to the Philistines' garrison that is on yonder side." But he did not tell his father. . . . 4 And between the passes by which Jonathan sought to cross over to the Philistines' garrison, there was a sharp crag on the one side, and a sharp crag on the other side, and the name of the one was Bozez, and the name of the other Seneh. 5 The one crag rose on the north opposite Michmash, and the other on the south opposite Geba. 6 Then Jonathan said to the young man who was carrying his armor, "Come and let us cross over to the garrison of these uncircumcised; perhaps the LORD will work for us, for the LORD is not restrained to save by many or by few." 7 And his armor bearer said to him, "Do all that is in your heart; turn yourself, and here I am with you according to your desire." 8 Then Jonathan said, "Behold, we will cross over to the men and reveal ourselves to them. 9 "If they say to us, 'Wait until we come to you'; then we will stand in our place and not go up to them. 10 "But if they say, 'Come up to us,' then we will go up, for the LORD has given them into our hands; and this shall be the sign to us." 11 And when both of them revealed themselves to the garrison of the Philistines, the Philistines said, "Behold, Hebrews are coming out of the holes where they have hidden themselves." 12 So the men of the garrison hailed Jonathan and his armor bearer and said, "Come up to us and we will tell you something." And Jonathan said to his armor bearer, "Come up after me, for the LORD has given them into the hands of Israel." 13 Then Jonathan climbed up on his hands and feet, with his armor bearer behind him; and they fell before Jonathan, and his armor bearer put some to death after him. 14 And that first slaughter which Jonathan and his armor bearer made was about twenty men within about half a furrow in an acre of land.*

Many years ago, a quiet and reserved friend of mine named Keith had become discouraged in his inability to land a good job. He had regretfully acquired a college degree with a very impractical major, and now saw himself vocationally doomed to struggle just to scrounge up a meager living for the wife and family he someday hoped to have. But Keith believed that the Lord had endowed him with a package of talents that obligated him to attempt something extraordinary. He announced at a prayer meeting that he was embarking on an attempt to be accepted at a law school and become an attorney. At first, some of the brethren thought that the quiet and laid back Keith had bitten off more than he could chew. But through prayer and counsel, Keith (like Jonathan) had become convinced that the Lord would have him *cross over*, thinking that *perhaps the Lord would work for him* and enable him to take a law degree *into his hands*.

The road of the law school application process was cluttered with challenging bulls, but Keith eventually grabbed every one of them by the horns. Acceptance finally came. Law school was exhausting and job placement grueling. But for over a decade now, Keith has labored as an attorney for a law firm in the Detroit area. He's become a pillar in his local church, and a source of invaluable legal counsel to many pastors in the Midwest.

A father with a teenage son may be reading these pages with sweaty palms. His son is nearing those critical high school days during the junior and senior year when important maneuvers ought to be made. Specific colleges ought to be researched and visited. But just opening up those glossy pamphlets and considering those sky-high tuition costs can make a Dad prematurely assess that for his son, the road to a reputable institution is financially impassable.

Here's where a father and a son have got to grab the bull by the horns. There are ways to make this work. Instead of passively sitting back and fretting, aggressively researching and "spying out the land" can pay off big time. Many web sites and publications are available to help. The Princeton Review publishes an annual edition of *Paying for College Without Going Broke*. The diligent hunter will discover that there are myriads of scholarship possibilities, financial aid packages, and work-study programs available to almost any student who earnestly seeks quality education.

Rudy Ruettinger was a young man from a lower class family in a steel mill town. He was determined to attend Notre Dame and play on its varsity football team. Everybody called him a foolish dreamer. In high school, he'd been a mediocre player and a sub par student, but he was driven to achieve his goal. Rudy hacked his way through a jungle of difficulties, from first studying at community college, to then getting academically accepted at ND, to earning enough money for tuition; to perspiring and bleeding his way onto the scrub scouting team. For the last home game of his senior year, he actually got the chance to suit up and wear a golden helmet. In the closing seconds of that game, he made a tackle that indelibly imprinted his name into ND football history. He was then carried off the field on his teammates' shoulders, all in the shadow of the golden dome. Simply put, he wouldn't be denied. Though everybody said, "There's no way!" Rudy, however, ***found*** a way.

That's the kind of resolution a man of God needs to muster up to achieve his goals related to vocational training for service to God. Though things may look academically or financially bleak, take a lesson from Nehemiah who inspired the downcast Jerusalemites into rebuilding the walls: "You see the bad situation we are in, that Jerusalem is desolate and its gates burned by fire. Come let us rebuild . . . the God of heaven will give us success" (Nehemiah 2:18-20).

Getting to college, of course, is only the beginning. Now it's time to generate academic sweat to "study to shew thyself approved unto God" (2 Timothy 2:15 KJV). Hopefully, in high school you've positioned yourself well with good study habits, and now in college you labor with all your might, for "Whether . . . you eat or drink or whatever you do, do all to the glory of God" (1 Corinthians 10:31).

I know that I've arbitrarily focused on the academic track of vocational training. The same aggressive dominion principles apply whether or not a college degree is in the picture. For example, a young man in our church early on saw that his best skills were in his hands, so he became an apprentice to a respectable drywall contractor. Over the years he learned the art to the point where he's become a master himself. He's gradually building up a clientele with after hours side jobs, and now he's on the verge of going "on his own" as a profitable drywall entrepreneur.

> **Proverbs 22:29** *Do you see a man skilled in his work? He will stand before kings; He will not stand before obscure men.*

Like the bleak primeval earth of Genesis 1, our youthful lives can appear "formless and void" (1:2). But it's a very God-honoring thing to imitate Him by making specific plans, and methodically executing them, that by His grace, we can look back and say that the results are "good," even "very good" (1:31).

With the God-ordained, manly-dominion viewpoint, a man can accomplish great things with his life.

In my reading of history, observing of life, and talking with influential people, I've come to a conviction about men of great accomplishment, those who stand head and shoulders above their peers. The chief factor of their greatness is not their IQ's; whether or not they're geniuses. It's not the issue of mental aptitude, competence, or ability. The chief greatness-producing trait is an aggressive dominion mindset. They refuse to be passive. They aren't "four-balls." They're "players." They ***find*** a way, and they ***do it***.

What about you?

Chapter 8
Job Hunting

Early on in college, Alan responsibly assessed his personal gifts and aptitudes, studied the job market nationwide, sought the input of wise counselors, and concluded that he'd pursue a career in the teaching profession. After his graduation ceremony, he held a very marketable teacher's certificate. But to his surprise and dismay, principals were not banging on his door, or calling on his phone asking him to join their schools. The initial resumes he'd sent out, and interviews he'd had, elicited no appealing responses or offers. These rejections delivered to Alan's confidence a devastating blow. "For four years I studied and worked my heart out, and now nobody's interested in my services!" Alan felt like curling up into a purple four-ball.

Jake had studied engineering at a major university. Right out of college he was snatched up by the automobile industry where he enjoyed great success. A few years later, a headhunter offered him a more desirable position in the furniture industry that he researched, eventually accepted, and thoroughly enjoyed. But then the economic recession of the late 1990's hit, and Jake was laid off. The much sought after Jake found himself to be the "no-one-seems-to-want-Jake." After many months of full-time job-hunting, and daily rejection, Jake found himself deflated, lacking courage, and becoming strangled with despair.

Unemployment can mentally, emotionally, and spiritually shake a man to his foundations. A man without work can become like waters without current. Standing water soon putrefies into a scummy pond. Jake battled with deep discouragement. Other men battle with other issues. When David should have been directing a war, he was roaming the roof. His unemployed mind became the stagnant waters for the growth of immoral bacteria. He ended up aimlessly gawking on his roof instead of attentively fighting his battle (2 Samuel 11:1-5, the Bathsheba debacle).

Thomas Steele writes:

> Indeed activity (of labor) is so natural and delightful to man, that if idleness had the sanction of a law to enforce it, no doubt many would willingly pay their fine for liberty to work. [1]

In situations like Alan and Jake's, it's peculiarly necessary to fight off passive-purple- four-ballism. What a daunting task it becomes just to get up, get dressed, and face another day. Who relishes the thought of facing another painful rejection? Who enjoys knocking on a prospective employer's door to be met again with the all too frequent bottom line: "Sorry, you're of no use to us."

Absorbing this kind of chronically painful treatment can result in half-hearted efforts and a subtle hiding-at-home pattern. A "well I'm praying about it" syndrome, or an "I'm seeking God's will" explanation may justify such encroaching passivity. And the stagnating waters putrefy all the more.

Our hearts can begin to echo the sentiments of the proverbial sluggard who says, "There is a lion outside; I shall be slain in the streets" (Proverbs 22:13). Out there is pain. In here, maybe even under the covers, is safety and security.

Here's where, so help us God, we've got to pluck up courage and do what the Apostle urges: ". . .act like men, be strong . . ." (1 Corinthians 16:13). The key quality of manhood to which Paul is referring here is that noble trait of courage.

This is the time for some holy self-talk: "The Lord has given me a mandate to subdue and rule. He's called me to *provide* for my family and *share* with my fellow men (Ephesians 4:28). My wife and my children are depending on me. Though there may be any number of lions out there, it's my assigned duty to get out there, face them, and slay them, so help me God!"

David's mighty man, Benaiah, inspires us here.

> **2 Samuel 23:20** *Then Benaiah the son of Jehoiada, the son of a valiant man of Kabzeel, who had done mighty deeds, . . . went down and killed a lion in the middle of a pit on a snowy day*

Apparently, a lion that had been driven into the neighborhood of human dwellings by a heavy fall of snow, had taken refuge in a cistern, endangering the lives of innocent passersby. Surely Benaiah had reluctant misgivings about single-handedly confronting this beast, but the footprints of duty and brotherly love led him down into that dangerous pit. His heroism in behalf of others has been preserved in printer's ink to inspire us to daily do the same.

After many months of pounding the pavement, networking with headhunters, and slaying bouts of roaring discouragement, Jake landed an adequate job, with an excellent company, in a highly desirable town—with a solid church. Though he personally labored hard toward this longed for goal, Jake continuously and wisely says, "This is God's doing and not mine!"

> **Proverbs 21:31** *The horse is prepared for the day of battle, but victory belongs to the Lord.*

In contrast, Alan, the teacher, has been quite passive and reluctant to expend himself and expose himself to rejection. Alan, as of now, remains without a fulltime job. Yes, victory belongs to the Lord, but we're responsible to adequately ***prepare*** the horse!

1 *The Religious Tradesman*, p.13

Chapter 9
Hard Working

During my days as a new believer, I attended a Christian college that was greatly used of the Lord for my good. I continue to thank God for that institution and its influence on my life. I do, however, remember an area of imbalanced teaching in the area of vocational labor. It appeared most strikingly in the chapel sessions. I can still see myself sitting in the bleachers of the college gymnasium listening carefully to speakers who oftentimes sought to direct youthful students into a field of "full-time Christian service," such as becoming a pastor or a missionary.

The message came through loud and clear: "If you really want to do something meaningful, something that will be of eternal value, something that will be sold out and pleasing to God, you'll dedicate your life to full-time kingdom service."

The flipside of this message also came through loud and clear: "If you don't dedicate your life to full-time Christian service, you won't be viewed by God as *sold out*, won't be doing something of eternal value, and won't be giving yourself to something that is really meaningful."

It was the "sacred vs. secular" dichotomy. Ministerial work is sacred and holy. Professional or vocational work is secular and worldly. As a result of this mentality, many Christians view their daily non-ministerial employment as relatively insignificant in the eyes of God. The Christian carpenter, accountant, or store manager too often sees his job as only a necessary means to the worldly end of financial survival.

The practical upshot is often a half-hearted pursuit of mediocrity in the work place.

The carpenter adequately plods along for years at framing houses for his boss, but his lack of ambition and creativity has made that same boss reluctant to elevate him up to the position of finishing off the interior areas like the kitchen or living room. The accountant does his work between the hours of nine and five, but his lack of ambition and initiative has caused him to often be passed over for a promotion. The store manager, though high in seniority, loses his job early during the recession because his lack of enthusiasm and motivation are evident to the owners.

Such mediocre endeavors may be subconsciously justified by the thought, "Well, at least I'm not worldly minded," or "Hey, I'm trying to avoid a carnal spirit."

The Bible teaches no such "sacred vs. secular" dichotomy when it comes to human endeavoring. Earthly labor of all kinds is presented as a very sacred activity. What could be more sacred than carrying out the Lord's personal assignment to us: "Be fruitful and multiply, and fill the earth, and subdue it and rule over the fish of the sea and over the birds of the sky, and over every living thing that moves on the earth" (Genesis 1:28)?

For Adam in particular this meant taking up the agricultural vocation of a farmer: "Then the Lord God took the man and put him into the garden of Eden to cultivate and keep it" (Genesis 2:15). For Adam, no more sacred activity could be conceived of than digging in the dirt, rearranging shrubs, and pruning vines. Since he was at his God-ordained post, his labors were blessedly consecrated and hallowed.

For us as image bearing men and women, our earthly vocations constitute an altar upon which we are to daily offer up the sacrifice of our choicest labor that it might send up a soothing aroma into the nostrils of our God. Psalm 104 provides the poetic account of creation. The earth is established, water covers it as a blanket, the mountains rise up, the vegetation sprouts, and the birds and beasts frolic. And with this altar having been set, man, the crown of God's creation, sets out daily to offer up his sacred act of worship:

Psalm 104:23 *Man goes forth to his work and to his labor until evening.*

Do you see yourself at the crack of dawn, with your hoe swung over your shoulder, heading out into the creation to offer up your daily sacrifice of God-honoring work? He deserves not the lame, sick, and blind of our flocks; not the half-hearted, mediocre, and feeble of our efforts. Rather he deserves our best.

> **Colossians 3:23** *Whatever you do, do your work heartily, as for the Lord rather than for men*

As a civil courtroom is a sacred place which requires from us conscientious truth telling, and as a married couple's bedroom is a sacred place which requires from them chaste loving, so too our workshops and offices are sacred places requiring from us diligent laboring. In these places of labor, we're sacredly obligated to reflect the character of the God who made us; the God who creatively labored for six days, pronouncing the final grade of His creation,"very good" (Genesis 1:31).

So, when we're faced with a knotty vocational challenge like our work team deteriorating into anarchy, or our desk swamped with tasks, or our assigned project falling apart into a chaotic mess, let's rise to the occasion. It's not time to curl up into a purple four-ball. It's time to reflect our beloved heavenly Father, who took the primeval chaos of the unformed universe, and with his efficient labor ordered it into a finely tuned domain over which He stood as a capable ruler.

A dear friend of mine works for a global auto interior manufacturer. He's a quality control troubleshooter. When a GM or Chrysler project encounters difficulties, Roy is called in to untie the Gordian knots in order to avert corporate disasters, and satisfy the irritated clients. One evening as we sat in his living room, Roy went on and on about the chaotic variables he had to work with. He told of machines breaking down, chemical formulas being improperly mixed, electrical circuitry being inadequately designed, and ground transportation not keeping schedules. As his voice reached a frustrated pitch, Roy looked at me and said, "But you know, Pastor, I love my job. At my work, I'm in my element. I love taking things that are broken and putting them back together. I love arriving at a mess and making things neat and clean again!"

For Roy, a week at work is more satisfying and fulfilling than would be a week at Disney World. So it should be. Just as an eagle has been given wings to fly; so man has been given hands to work. Our work is our blue sky!

Do you see why we ought to have a skip in our step when we, near dawn, with our hoes slung over our shoulders, exit our homes? We're heading out into the wonderland of creation, to "go forth to our work, to our labor until evening" (Psalm 104:23). What a privilege! Such should be our enthused attitude whenever we venture out into our God-appointed and sacred plots of the garden. Such an aggressive, subduing, and hard-working spirit is very glorifying to our God whom we're obligated to hourly image. In the Trinity Hymnal (#444), we find these words by Anna L. Waring:

> I ask Thee for the daily strength, to none that asked denied,
> A mind to blend with outward life, while keeping at Thy side,
> Content to fill a little space, if Thou be glorified.

This kind of hard-working ethic not only gives glory to God, but also typically issues in dividends to the conscientious and inspired worker, which involve a raise in salary, promotion in position, and well-deserved esteem in the eyes of God and men (Proverbs 22:29).

Chapter 10
Financial Earning

Make all you can. Save all you can.
Give all you can.

This is a famous quote of *John Wesley* regarding his view of a godly perspective toward work and money. He clearly encouraged holy ambition in vocational labor with an eye toward the financial harvest.

The Bible does the same.

> **Proverbs 10:4** *Poor is he who works with a negligent hand, But the hand of the diligent <u>makes rich</u>.*

Now, don't misunderstand. God's word does not teach us that earning money is an atheistic enterprise achieved by aggressive men who are able to earn large piles of cash by the sweat of their own brows. Eighteen verses later, the endeavor of wealth accumulating is placed in the context of God's sovereignty.

> **Proverbs 10:22** *It is the blessing of the LORD that <u>makes rich</u>, And He adds no sorrow to it.*

Put the two passages together, and we learn that the Lord financially blesses hard-working people. Further, the end of being "made rich" is not presented as a carnal cursing, but a holy blessing. The reception of a handsome financial profit in the long run is presented as a godly incentive toward diligent laboring in the short run.

I suppose that some sincere readers at this point may feel very uncomfortable. Some may be thinking, "Oh, this appeal to making large sums of money in our work sounds so carnal! Doesn't Paul teach us,

"And if we have food and covering, with these we shall be content" (1 Timothy 6:8)?

Yes, certainly we must steer clear of the sin of covetousness. *But simply because a principle is pervertable, does not mean that it's disposable*. Simply because a child may be abused by spanking doesn't mean that we should dispose of spanking. Simply because aggressive profit making can degenerate into covetousness doesn't mean that we should dispose of aggressive profit making.

Could it be that for some, the discomfort toward aggressive profit making stems from a discomfort toward hard work? Could it be that for some, the charge of worldliness regarding this theme actually stems from a passive-purple-four-ball aversion to hard work? After all, it's much easier for a five-talent man to bury some of his abilities in a hole of slothfulness, than for him to conscientiously invest all of his talents for the benefit of his Master.

> Whatever sagacity of mind, depth of judgment, or quickness of invention you are endowed with, should be employed. . . . Have you a firm constitution, a vigorous nerve, an able arm, or a curious hand? Serve God with these in your callings. For to this end were you entrusted with them.[1]

Sean may work as an electrician for a construction company and make an adequate wage providing food and covering for his wife and children. He knows that he could receive a handsome salary increase if he'd become certified as a journeyman. But that would require many months of diligently burning midnight oil to study and pass the required series of tests. But after a long day at work, and putting the kids to bed, he loves to plop in front of the television set watching sports or the history channel for a couple of hours. In these circumstances, Sean may even silence his squealing conscience with muzzling thoughts about how he's acting as a man of tranquil and godly contentment.

John Murray, in discussing the creation ordinance of labor, warns against the danger of "idleness" putting on the "garb of piety" by considering labor as "incompatible with the demands of communion with God." In this context, he quotes 1 Timothy 5:8: "But if anyone does not provide for his own, and especially for those of his own household, he has denied the faith, and is worse than an unbeliever."[2]

Sean's family, both immediate (i.e., his children) and extended (i.e., his widowed mother), could be greatly benefited by his wage increase. Further, his increased giving could positively enhance Sean's church and its kingdom endeavors.

God has mightily used the accumulation of financial resources into the hands of a godly man throughout redemptive history. Abraham's financial muscle (318 trained men) was harnessed to rescue Lot and his family from the five king confederacy that terrorized Sodom (see Genesis 14). Job's economic wealth was used to help poor orphans, make widows' hearts sing, and break the jaws of the wicked (see Job 1:1-3; 29:11-20). Boaz' agricultural prosperity formed the wings of refuge under which Ruth and Naomi found shelter (cf. Ruth 2:1, 12; 3:9; 4:6). Barzillai the Gileadite single-handedly sustained David's entourage in the wilderness during the Absalom uprising (cf. 2 Samuel 17:27-29; 19:32). Joanna and Susanna contributed large portions of their wealth to support the ministry of our Lord Jesus (see Luke 8:1-3). Joseph of Arimathea, a wealthy man, influenced the paranoid Pilate to permit Christ's body to be taken down from the cross and lain in his own expensive tomb, providing a suitable stage for the resurrection spectacle (cf. Matthew 27:57-60). Frederick of Saxony flexed his affluence by securing a safe hiding place at the Wartburg Castle for the endangered reformer Martin Luther.

All of these examples practically demonstrate the principle taught by the Apostle Paul in 1 Timothy 6:17-19:

> *Instruct those who are rich in this present world not to be conceited or to fix their hope on the uncertainty of riches, but on God, who richly supplies us with all things to enjoy. 18 Instruct them to do good, to be rich in good works, to be generous and ready to share, 19 storing up for themselves the treasure of a good foundation for the future, so that they may take hold of that which is life indeed.*

The Lord has wonderfully equipped a large portion of the Body of Christ with brilliant minds and skilled hands that they might use these talents in the business world to the end of their producing financial dividends that will support expensive kingdom endeavors. Sadly, some of these choice servants of Christ have abandoned their fields of expertise and instead have tried to force-fit themselves into ministries because misguided teachers have denigrated the importance of *non-ministry* vocations.

I would not belittle the glorious vocation of the pastor or the missionary. Would to God, that He would send out many who read these pages into the ministerial fields that are white unto harvest. But in the *body* of Christ, we are not all *mouths*, fashioned to give ourselves full-time to the oral declaration of the gospel. Many of us are *thighs*, fashioned to generate the financial muscle, so that the *mouths* can be carried to the four corners of the earth with the gospel.

Though carnal sounding, *cash is the fuel that runs the kingdom machinery*. Many kingdom ships that could be launched, end up rotting in the harbor due to lack of funds. Were it not for generous financial supporters, the great missionary Adoniram Judson would never have set sail for Burma.

Robert Louis Dabney writes on using our work-generated property for the cause of the kingdom of God:

> We are to serve God with all our strength. Our property is a part of our strength, and therefore we are to serve Him with all our property... There are so many thousand thirsty channels in which our benevolence might flow.[3]

Dabney further adds:

> We must be distinguished for our large-hearted liberality and our expanded plans of beneficence... We must burst forth on every side into a magnificence of missionary enterprise, as marvelous as the growth of our commerce, arts, agriculture, and general prosperity... And hence it is the time for the church to go forward with gigantic strides, and give tenfold expansion to all those means for glorifying God which his temporal bounties can sustain.[4]

Financial fuel for the kingdom machinery does not spontaneously rain down from heaven. It must be *drilled for* and *pumped out* by hard-working, enterprising men. In my own town of Holland, Michigan, a man named Ed Prince, decades ago, began a small business in his garage. He based his company's philosophy on the biblical work ethic and Christian values. The Lord prospered his aggressive labors and by the 1980's Prince Corporation had risen to become a world-class auto interior manufacturer.

Throughout the years, hundreds of Christian organizations were financially fueled by the deep wells of Mr. Prince's economic prosperity. In Washington, D.C., the *Family Research Council's* headquarters was built with funds donated by Mr. Prince. My own church, The Reformed Baptist Church of Holland, enjoys its handsome and spacious red-bricked, white-pillared building due, humanly speaking, to a generous bequest from the Prince family property holdings.

At the funeral of Ed Prince, a close friend of his succinctly eulogized the life of this enterprising Christian man: "The life of Ed Prince moved mountains of evil."

Now, what kind of men does the Lord use to such mountain moving ends? He does not use passive-purple-four-ball men. He uses aggressive, hard-working, enterprising, dominion-minded men. It's such choice servants that the Lord harnesses for the great work of gospel proclamation and kingdom extension.

Surely, very few of us will be so providentially positioned as was Ed Prince to strike it rich with such a deep and bubbling up oil field. But we can each be like one of those small, hard-working oil rigs that we occasionally see alongside the interstate; pumping hard, making our important contribution to the thirsty kingdom machinery.

Over the past decade and a half, I've been involved in a number of endeavors to plant churches in Canada and the U.S. As a result, the North American map is now dotted with a number of young and thriving congregations. But humanly speaking, many of these dots would not be there today, had it not been for strategically placed, hard-working men whose hands had been blessed with prosperity. In one town, a flourishing agricultural related entrepreneur financially enabled the fledgling church to call and support its first pastor. In another city, a savvy stockbroker's tithes and offerings made the little work monetarily viable. In yet another place, two enterprising civil engineers carried a lion's share of the early financial weight.

Other church plants, due to a preponderance of lower paid givers, have struggled for years without being able to call a fully supported pastor. This has greatly hindered their ability to establish their ministries in their communities. Some have withered on the vine and died.

Churches that do enjoy fully supported pastors remain somewhat handicapped in their ministry due to their inability to acquire a permanent building for their meeting places. Due to financial constraints, they're forced to utilize short-term rental arrangements that sometimes force them to move to and fro like wandering gypsies. This does not engender confidence in visitors who are looking for a stable church situation.

So, in view of these things, I think John Wesley's motto is profound:

> "Make all you can. Save all you can. Give all you can."

Passive-purple-four-ballism won't get it done. Aggressive, manly dominion, blessed by the Lord, will.

10 / FINANCIAL EARNING

1 *The Religious Tradesman*, p.73
2 John Murray, *Principles of Conduct* (Grand Rapids: Eerdmans, 1978), pp.84-85
3 Robert Louis Dabney, *Discussions of Robert Louis Dabney, Vol. 1*, "Principles of Christian Economy" (Edinburgh: Banner of Truth Trust, 1891), p.3
4 Dabney, Vol. 1, "Our Secular Prosperity," pp.704-705

Chapter 11
Manly Dominion in Decision Making: Impressions

The womb of our life motions is found in our thinking. A man's pattern of thinking gives birth either to passive living or aggressive living. Continuously, we're confronted with practical decisions:

Should I take this job?
Should I buy this home?
Should I move to this city?
Should I attend this school?
Should I join this church?
Should I confront this brother?
Should I continue this relationship?
Should I face my son head on about this habit?

Haddon Robinson writes:

> Sacred cows make the best hamburger, but the meat can be hard to swallow.
>
> Christians cherish a mythology that, along with their theology, shapes and directs their lives. Perhaps no myth more strongly influences us than our understanding of *how to know the will of God*. We want to make right decisions, for we realize that the decisions we make turn around and make us. As we choose one end of the road, we choose

> another. When we select a life's work, a life's partner, or a college, we desire God's direction in those choices....
>
> If we ask, "How can I know the will of God?" we may be asking the wrong question. The Scriptures do not command us to find God's will for most of life's choices nor do we have any passage instructing on how it can be determined. Equally significant, the Christian community has never agreed on how God provides us with such special revelation. *Yet we persist in searching for God's will because decisions require thought and sap energy. We seek relief from the responsibility of decision-making and we feel less threatened by being passive rather than active when making important choices.* (Emphasis mine)[1]

I'm reminded of a college classmate of mine who had established a firewood business. Chad was an aggressive entrepreneur who during his college years owned his own house and rented out its rooms to fellow students. Through these business endeavors, Chad was paying his own way through Bible school, as he aspired to become a pastor. One afternoon, as we sat studying in the library, he confided in me about his frustration with an unnamed fellow student he had employed as a hired hand.

"We drove the truck up to the wooded area. I got out, unloaded the chain saws and equipment, and headed toward the trees. My man didn't follow. After a while, I returned to the truck and asked him, 'What's the matter?' He said, 'Don't you think we should first pray and ask God which tree we should cut down first?' Have you ever heard the saying, *He's so heavenly minded that he's no earthly good*?"

This hired hand's approach to life may sound very spiritual, but I believe it's typically nothing more than a misguided, passive-purple-four-ballism. A hyper-spiritual, unbiblical view of decision making cripples many believers with thought patterns that result in unwarranted delay and vacillation on the one hand, and irresponsible, impulsive, emotionally loaded judgments on the other.

We would do well to apply the principles of manly dominion to our patterns of decision making.

In Chapters 11-13 we'll focus on *Debunking Pop Perspectives.* Over the years, an elaborate folk theology of divine guidance has evolved in certain Christian circles. Its principles sound very spiritual, but in reality they're very unbiblical. They hold millions of minds in a passive straight jacket. Much of the faulty thinking revolves around the three themes of *Impressions*, *Circumstances*, and *Peace*.

In Chapters 14-15, we'll focus on *Highlighting Wise Principles*. There we'll describe a general path of wisdom for godly decision-making.

Impressions

Many Christians believe and teach that the most spiritual way of directing your life is by sensitively submitting to the *impressions* given to you by the Holy Spirit. These *impressions*, they say, may come in the form of *a quiet inner voice, an inward urging, and a heart compulsion. Impressions* may move a person to say, "I felt led to . . ."

If I might visually depict *impression* theology, think of a windsock on a country airstrip. That light fabric tube hangs lithely in the wind, submissively turning in the direction of the slightest breeze. That, says the *impressionist*, is the way a spiritual Christian will feel the mysterious blowing of the Spirit within his soul. This, we're told, is living the ideal life of communion with God.

A number of years ago we were selling our family home with a "For Sale by Owner" strategy. Early one evening, a delightful woman knocked at our door. She was so excited to see the "For Sale" sign in our front yard, and doubly thrilled to see that, by all appearances, our house matched nicely with her personal checklist. When she discovered that we were Christians, she bubbled out, "The Holy Spirit told me to drive down your street." When I asked what she meant by that, she said, "Oh, you know when He just tells you to take a different way home from work?" I quickly understood that she was a woman who made many of her decisions by *impressions*.

If I had asked this woman for a biblical justification for this style of decision-making, I assume she might have cited Acts 8 where "an angel of the Lord spoke to Philip saying, 'Arise and go south to the road that descends from Jerusalem to Gaza'" (v.26). Then, upon observing an Ethiopian eunuch in a chariot, "the Spirit said to Philip, 'Go up and join this chariot.'"(v.29)

I was once reading an article about a Christian's duty to evangelize. The pastor who authored the article divulged how one afternoon he was studying in his office when: "I was given a strong impression to go and visit the hospital." Not sure why he was there, he began to stroll the halls. Soon he met a woman, struck up a conversation with her, and was able to give her the gospel! These anecdotes led me to wonder what I'm to do when I'm dutifully keeping my nose to the studying grindstone, but feel like I'd rather be anywhere but here, chained to this chair and desk. I bet I could find someone to witness to at the golf course! Typically for me, such feelings are simply strong aversions to staying on an irksome task. *Impressions* and *feelings* are interesting things, aren't they?

Under it all, most impression-directed folks believe that *we're most spiritually minded when our decisions are based, not on the logical and rational, but on the emotional and mystical.* This way, they believe, we're most sensitive to God's personal disclosures of His will to us.

Let's admit it, we all fall into this once in a while. One evening I was driving home with my eyes open for a used bicycle for sale on a lawn or at a garage sale, since my son had outgrown his. Then it came over me: a *hunch*. I had a *hunch* that if I turned down this out-of-the-way side street, I'd find a great deal on a bike. I went with the *hunch*. I prayerfully drove down the street, wondering what the Lord might show me. I went to the end and back. There was no bike. The Lord showed me that *hunches* are *hunches* and not disclosures of direct revelation from Him!

> For every *hunch* that turns out to be correct there are many more which do not. "That people have *hunches* is obvious," writes Paul Wooley: "That many of them work out very well and others quite poorly is also obvious." But only the successful ones are related.[2]

Here's the fundamental problem with making decisions based on impressions. A decision-making model based on impressions relies on the expectation that God is still in the business of directly imparting new, *special revelation* to His people. Yes, asking God for life directing impressions, is asking God for fresh *special revelations*. This, I believe, is wrong and unbiblical.

We no longer live in the Apostolic age where the Lord was directing his church by dreams, visions, signs and wonders as he led Philip. In those early first century days, the Lord led His infant church by *miraculous* methods (Acts 8:26).

> **2 Corinthians 12:12** *The signs of a true apostle were performed among you with all perseverance, by signs and wonders and miracles.*

But the apostles died off by the end of the first century, and with them perished the miraculous direction by special revelations. The writer of Hebrews says as much as he speaks of our great salvation in Christ:

> **Hebrews 2:3-4** *How shall we escape, if we neglect so great salvation; which at the first began to be spoken by the Lord, and was confirmed unto us by them that heard him; (i.e. the apostles) 4 God also bearing them witness, both with signs and wonders, and with divers miracles, and gifts of the Holy Ghost, according to his own will?*

Being supernaturally directed by dreams, visions, and voices was an experience enjoyed by those in the Apostolic age. But the Apostles died away, and so too has this supernatural *new revelation* method died away.

Echoing the *Westminster Confession of Faith*, the *Second London Baptist Confession of Faith of 1689* well summarizes the issue in its very first chapter {chapter 1, paragraph 1}, which lays as the cornerstone the sufficiency of the Holy Scriptures:

> *The Holy Scripture is the only sufficient, certain, and infallible rule of all saving knowledge, faith, and obedience*, although the light of nature, and the works of creation and providence do so far manifest the goodness, wisdom, and power of God, as to leave men inexcusable; yet are they not sufficient to give that knowledge of God and his will which is necessary unto salvation. Therefore *it pleased the Lord at sundry times and in diverse manners to reveal himself, and to declare that his will unto his church*; and afterward *for the better preserving and propagating of the truth, and for the more sure establishment and comfort of the church* against the corruption of the flesh, and the malice of Satan, and the world, *to commit the same wholly unto writing*; *which maketh the Holy Scriptures to be the most necessary, those former ways of God's revealing his will unto his people being now ceased* [Emphasis mine].

Now, unlike in the Apostolic age, we have a better and superior revelation from God; the completed collection (canon) of the Holy Scriptures from Genesis to Revelation. God's word in our bibles provides us with all the revelation we need to discern God's will and make godly decisions. We should look no further for additional *disclosures* or *whisperings* or *words* from God.

John Murray insightfully writes,

> We may still fall into the error of thinking that while the Holy Spirit does not provide us with special revelations in the form of words or visions or dreams, yet he may and does provide us with some *direct feeling* or *impression* or conviction which we are to regard as the Holy Spirit's *intimation* to us of what his mind and will is in a particular situation. The present writer maintains that this view of the Holy Spirit's guidance amounts, in effect, to the same thing as to believe that the Holy Spirit gives *special revelation*. And the reason for this conclusion is that we are, in such an event, conceiving of the Holy Spirit as giving us some special and direct communication, be it in the form of feeling, *impression*, or conviction, a communication or intimation or direction that is not mediated to us through those means which God has ordained for our direction and guidance (i.e. the Scripture).[3]

The possession of the Scriptures makes the Christian *adequate for every good work*. By studying them, consulting them, meditating on them, praying over them, and thinking through their implications, I have all that I need to make wise decisions regarding which city I live in, which home I purchase, which job I accept, which person I marry, etc. They equip me for "every good work" (2 Timothy 3:16).

Without this foundational understanding of the sufficiency of the Scripture, many souls are tossed to and fro by every wind of feeling, emotion, and *hunch*. The Scriptures are able to make simple people wise.

> **Psalm 19:7** *The law of the LORD is perfect, restoring the soul; The testimony of the LORD is sure, making wise the simple.*

> **Psalm 119:99** *I have more insight than all my teachers, For Thy testimonies are my meditation.*

That's why the blessed man meditates on the Scriptures day and night (Psalm 1:1), carefully thinking through their themes and implications. But the *impression* model of decision making discourages the need for rigorous and serious thinking by suspending the mind and detouring the intellect. Again, listen to Donald Macloed:

> "God's promises of guidance are not given to save us the bother of thinking," writes John Stott. Sadly many Christians seem to think it is. As they plead for guidance what they are really looking for is a way of knowing God's will which dispenses with the need for disciplined and rigorous thought. They not only want absolute, revelational certainty. They want it painlessly, in some overwhelming, supernatural flash.[4]

In contrast, the New Testament insists on our aggressively employing our minds:

> **Romans 12:2** *Be transformed by the renewing of your mind...*

> **Ephesians 4:23** *Be renewed in the spirit of your mind...*

> **1 Peter 1:13** *...prepare your minds for action...*

Don't let the misguided folk theology of *impressions* turn you into an indecisive, unthinking, unbiblical, passive-purple four-ball.

1 *Forward* to Gary Freisen's book, *Decision Making and the Will of God* (Portland, OR: Multnomah Press, 1980), p.13
2 Donald Macleod, *The Spirit of Promise* (Houston: Christian Focus Publications, 1986; reprinted 1988), p.80
3 John Murray, *The Collected Writings of John Murray, Vol.1* (Edinburgh: Banner of Truth, 1970), p.187
4 op. cit., p.64

Chapter 12
Providence

A number of years ago, I was one of four pastors in a large, flourishing church in Grand Rapids, Michigan. A group of families were driving a long distance from the west, near the town of Holland. These families agreed to pioneer a church plant, as long as one of their pastors would come along with them. I became the privileged pastor who was asked to move into the Holland area.

As my wife and I approached the move, we were faced with the decision of housing. Where should we live? We continuously laid this matter before the Lord in prayer, while carefully evaluating our financial resources along with our family needs.

We established a sober-minded price range. We assessed that our five children needed adequate elbowroom, especially since we were a homeschool family. In the house would be my pastor's study. We also felt that our home should be well suited for hospitality and hosting overnight guests. When we put all of these things on paper, they translated into a very large house with a lot of square footage.

As we began to research the tight housing market in the Holland area, we discovered that in general, large houses were built with opulent extras, which translated into exorbitantly high prices. After much prayer and counsel, we decided to build a large, but modest, home on a flat, three-acre parcel of farmland. This plan enabled us to acquire a nonessential, but highly desirable, soccer/baseball field in the backyard. After all, we have four boys!

We purchased the land, secured a builder and drew up plans. But while I was sitting in the banker's office, presenting to him the drawings and financial figures, I realized that a misunderstanding had arisen between myself and the builder, resulting in a total price $21,000 higher than I had expected. This was very unsettling since we were shortly scheduled to set out on a two-week family vacation. While I was sharing this calamity with a dear adviser, she said, "Maybe the Lord is trying to tell you something. Maybe He's trying to tell you that you shouldn't build."

In response, I thought: "Could this really be so? We've prayed. We've researched. We've calculated. We've sought seasoned counsel. We've prayed and prayed. We've enjoyed many circumstantial encouragements. Am I wise to interpret this frustrating obstacle as the voice of God telling me that I should scrap the weeks of careful planning? Is a cross *providence*, a closed door like this, a decisive negative indicator in godly decision making?"

On the strength of my previously built decision, I pressed on with alternative endeavors to build the same house on the same property. Through the blessing of God, I contacted another builder with whom I had previously talked. He told me he had hit an unexpected lull and would like to make a bid. I showed him the plans, and within twenty-four hours he made a bid that would build the same house with the same quality materials for over $21,000 less than the original builder's quote.

For nearly a decade now, we've enjoyed the home, the pastor's study, the elbowroom, and yes, the grassy soccer field! For all of these kind gifts, we thank the Lord.

Here's the upshot: We must not make *circumstances* (providence) *the* decisive variable in decision making. It's not wise to read the favorable or unfavorable circumstances as necessarily the approval or disapproval of God. Providence is ambiguous, and is able to be interpreted in multiple ways.

We must not permit ourselves to be pushed around like passive-purple four-balls by the blows that events of providence bring our way. Instead, we should set a course based on the principles of Scripture, thoughtfully and prayerfully applied to the realities of daily living.

Many unconsciously hold to a contrary, more passive view. They feel that careful, logical deliberation and strategic preparation smack of carnality. In contrast, they feel that reading God's signposts in *providence* is the essence of spirituality. They believe God reveals his will to us by opening or closing doors in our paths. They consider that the spiritually sensitive Christian will not "lean on his own understanding" but instead "trust in the Lord" by sensitively submitting to the

Lord's providential orderings. This is the way many seek to *find God's will.*

"I sent in my job application to XYZ Inc., but since I haven't heard anything yet, it's clear that God has closed that door." That's an easy way to absolve oneself of the responsibility of diligently following up on a job opportunity with repeated and potentially embarrassing visits, calls and emails.

A seminary graduate says, "I know that my family is a mess right now, and my addiction to Internet pornography tears apart my conscience, but the fact that a church has just called me to be their pastor indicates to me that it must be *of the Lord.*" Don't bother him with God's written Word that clearly says, "an overseer must be . . . above reproach . . . one who manages his own household well . . . "(1 Timothy 3:1-7).

A shy young man is interested in a young woman. He stands over the telephone, reluctant to call her and make himself vulnerable to her rejecting his overtures. He lays out a fleece of sorts. "Lord, if the phone is busy or she's not home, I'll take it as your saying that now is not the time for me to pursue a relationship with her."

Such examples reflect an unbiblical, unthinking, anti-dominion mindset. Yes, it's true that providence makes up one important variable in a wise decision-making formula. But in godly decision making, providence itself is not necessarily decisive.

Think of Jonah. God's word tells him to go to Nineveh. He chafes under this word and instead chooses to head in the other direction for Tarshish.

> **Jonah 1:3** *But Jonah rose up to flee to Tarshish from the presence of the LORD. So he went down to Joppa, found a ship which was going to Tarshish, paid the fare, and went down into it to go with them to Tarshish from the presence of the LORD.*

Look at this. Jonah enjoyed a smooth journey to Joppa, found a ship about to depart to this rare destination, discovered that a hammock was available on board, and was blessed with a fair wind westward! Surely the open door *circumstances* of *providence* indicate that it must be *of the Lord*, right? Was Jonah right to think he was therefore doing the right thing? No way! He was in actuality defiantly opposing God.

O. Palmer Robertson writes:

> Sometimes when everything is going just right, you conclude that God's hand must be in it. But that may not be the case at all. You need something more specific than *circumstances*. You need the confirmation of the word of God...How many times in your life have you gone against the teaching of the word of God because you had tunnel vision and stubbornly saw only what you wanted? Beware of reading *providential circumstances* in a way that contradicts the explicit commands of God.[1]

Direction for life is not found in passively watching the ambiguous winds of *providence*. We aren't to navigate our lives simply by observing which doors of circumstance are open for our pressing on and which doors are closed for our backing down.

That's not how the Apostle Paul lived. In Romans 1:13, he writes:

> *And I do not want you to be unaware, brethren, that often I have planned to come to you (and have been prevented thus far) in order that I might obtain some fruit among you also, even as among the rest of the Gentiles.*

But Paul didn't see a closed door as a "no" answer from the Lord. If he deemed his plan a wise one, he continued to knock on the door.

> **Romans 15:22-24** *For this reason I have often been hindered from coming to you; 23 but now, with no further place for me in these regions, and since I have had for many years a longing to come to you 24 whenever I go to Spain— for I hope to see you in passing, and to be helped on my way there by you, when I have first enjoyed your company for a while—*

Interestingly, though Christians today speak of doors that are *closed*, Scripture does not. The need for open doors certainly implies the existence of some that are closed. But that doesn't seem to be the mentality of Paul. If he was sovereignly prevented from pursuing a plan, and yet the plan itself was sound, he simply waited and tried again later. He did not view a blocked endeavor as a *closed-door* sign from God that his plan was faulty. He accepted the fact that he could not pursue that plan *at that time*. Yet he continued to desire, pray, and plan for the eventual accomplishment of the goal.[2]

Further, who's to say that the "openness" or "shutness" of a door is the hand of *God* telling us which way we should to go (1 Thessalonians 2:18)?

We can be tempted to use *circumstances* as a way to cop out of difficult projects and gut-wrenching decisions. Remember when Nehemiah made his discouraging night ride through the rubble of a Jerusalem he was hoping to repair? The circumstances were far worse than he had imagined or planned for.

> **Nehemiah 2:13-15** *So I went out at night by the Valley Gate in the direction of the Dragon's Well and on to the Refuse Gate, inspecting the walls of Jerusalem which were broken down and its gates which were consumed by fire. 14 Then I passed on to the Fountain Gate and the King's Pool, but there was no place for my mount to pass. 15 So I went up at night by the ravine and inspected the wall. Then I entered the Valley Gate again and returned.*

Look, a closed door! Upon telling of this frustrating obstacle to a dear friend, Nehemiah might have heard these words: "Maybe the Lord is trying to tell you something. Maybe He's trying to tell you that you shouldn't build." With such a suggestion, I think Nehemiah would not have agreed. He didn't live his life as a passive four-ball. Rather, he lived on Scriptural principle; and when it was in his lawful power, he bulldozed through barricading obstacles.

During the year between my college and seminary training, I got a job as a letter carrier for the US Postal Service. This enabled me to further stockpile savings so that I could responsibly marry my fianceé, Dianne. As September and seminary neared, it seemed evident I'd have to lose my excellent wage and generous benefits package. Seminary classes were in the day—so was mail delivery. The Post Office policy (not written law) was clear: *stay full time or quit.* Part time employment was not an option. The door was closed. Dianne and I prayed that the Lord would direct us to a profitable and flexible part-time job.

One early August afternoon while delivering mail, I formulated a plan. Maybe I could work evening special delivery shifts a couple nights per week, carry mail on Saturday, and slip in a partial shift somewhere else during the week. I thought it was worth a try. Praying like Nehemiah before Artaxerxes, I stood before my supervisor who told me he thought it was an impossible idea. "I can't tailor-make a special schedule just for you. The union would have a fit."

So I went to his supervisor, in whose eyes I saw a slight glimmer when I told him my plan. He said he was willing to give it a try, but couldn't approve of it unless the assistant Postmaster gave the green light. His last words were: "Don't let the union hear anything about this."

After a long talk, the assistant Postmaster said, "Okay, Chanski, I'm willing to give it a try; but make sure you keep a low profile. If they find out we're giving you a special schedule, you'll be gone." For the next two years I worked a tailor-made schedule and enjoyed the excellent wages and the great benefits, which covered the birth expenses of our first-born. No one ever noticed or objected to the strangeness of my schedule. The Lord was a hedge of protection around me.

Though the door was at first slammed shut, a decision to keep knocking, or even cut a new doorway, was blessed by God, resulting in a windfall to our young family.

Again, man is to exercise dominion by an aggressive subduing of his environment; his *circumstances.* In decision-making we must not adopt an unscriptural, mystical model that results in our passively permitting ourselves to be pushed around by our environment—like a four-ball. Instead, in circumstances where we are biblically allowed and authorized to press forward, let us humbly, prayerfully, and aggressively seek to do the pushing around.

12 / PROVIDENCE

1 Jonah, *A Study in Compassion* (Edinburgh: Banner of Truth, 1990), p.17
2 *Decision Making and the Will of God*, p.80

Chapter 13
Peace

Holland, Michigan is located on the shore of the Great Lake Michigan. Our church building is very close to Lake Macatawa, an inland lake that enjoys a deep channel access out to the big lake. Pleasure boats as well as ocean-going freighters move back and forth between the big and little lake. Often a pleasure boat will venture out into the potentially treacherous Great Lake and become overwhelmed by fog. Since the visual indicators of sun, stars or horizon become obscured, the captain must resort to his compass. He knows that if he heads due east, he'll eventually hit the Michigan Shoreline, which he can follow back into the harbor.

Likewise, in decision making, we can feel overwhelmed as if by a fog. The swarming details can cloud up our thinking. It's here that many make a mistake by abandoning the instrument of *biblical thinking*, and take up the compass of *mystical feeling*. In difficult situations of life, many resort to being passively led by "inner peace" rather than by *biblical principle* prayerfully and prudently applied.

Dorothy has been married a number of years to a man whom she now believes she never really loved. For months, she's been struggling internally regarding what she should do with her marriage. She's prayed, read her bible, sought counsel, and wrestled hard over this issue. Finally, she sits down with a spiritual adviser and says, "I've come to the conclusion that I should divorce him. I know that I have no biblical grounds. He hasn't committed fornication or abandoned me. But I know it's God's will because He's *given me such a peace about it.*" This really happened! For Dorothy, *inner peace* became her trusted compass, her final arbiter, and her priority card that trumped all others.

Dorothy's view on *inner peace* isn't uncommon. Many believe that the Holy Spirit brings *peace* to our hearts when we are in the *center* of God's will. In contrast, it is believed that when we experience *restlessness* and inward *anxiety*, we've begun moving in the wrong direction. In a nutshell, it's believed that God leads and directs us by *mystically manipulating our feelings* toward or away from a tranquil sensation of *peace*. This view is commonly supported by a passage like Colossians 3:15:

> *And let the peace of Christ rule in your hearts, to which indeed you were called in one body; and be thankful.*

"There you have it," says a superficial Bible reader, "I'm supposed to let *peace rule* in my life. That means *peace* is to be the final *arbiter* or *umpire* when it comes to decision-making."

But a careful examination of this passage reveals that the *peace* referred to here is not inward peace of the soul, but outward peace with other believers. As 3:15b indicates, it is *peace* within the body of the church that is in view. The preceding context makes this equally clear:

> **Colossians 3:12-14** *And so, as those who have been chosen of God, holy and beloved, put on a heart of compassion, kindness, humility, gentleness and patience; 13 bearing with one another, and forgiving each other, whoever has a complaint against anyone; just as the Lord forgave you, so also should you. 14 And beyond all these things put on love, which is the perfect bond of unity.*

The peace called for in Colossians 3:15, is not *personal tranquility* of heart, but *corporate tranquility* of the church. Let interpersonal peace and not hostility reign in your hearts toward one another as you live as humble peacemakers (Matthew 5:9), in the bond of unity. This passage is not at all referring to an internal compass for decision-making.

Paul does also speak of *the peace of God which surpasses all comprehension.*

Philippians 4:6-7 *Be anxious for nothing, but in everything by prayer and supplication with thanksgiving let your requests be made known to God. 7 And the peace of God, which surpasses all comprehension, shall guard your hearts and your minds in Christ Jesus.*

But this is also not presented as an internal compass for decision-making. It refers to the tranquility of heart enjoyed by the believer who hides his hell deserving soul "in Christ Jesus."

> This inward peace is bestowed on the basis of Christ's objective achievement, for *peace* from God is found upon the work of reconciliation that established peace with God [Romans 5:1; Ephesians 2:14ff].[1]

Again, an internal compass for decision making is not in view.

Now, there certainly is an internal compass of sorts to which a man must remain very sensitive. It's called the *conscience. Conscience* functions as a moral sheriff. *Conscience* urges a man to do that which he regards as right, and urges him against that which he regards as wrong (Romans 2:14-15). In the Christian, the Holy Spirit sets up residence in the conscience and holds a powerful sway. The believer is to make sure that he does not "grieve the Holy Spirit"(Ephesians 4:30). He must submit to the Spirit's *strivings* within his conscience. But if certain felt *strivings* and *urgings* are not in keeping with the written Word of God, the believer can be sure it's not the Work of the Holy Spirit.

Dorothy's *peace* in pursuing an unbiblical divorce was clearly not the work of the Holy Spirit, because her decided course was in diametric opposition to the Scripture, which has been authored by the Holy Spirit. The written Word is the authoritative judge that should validate or cancel any felt sense of *peace*. Dorothy's *peace* may have been due to a treaty she'd deceitfully made with her selfish lusts.

So again, we return to the objective revelation of the Bible. It's upon this written rock that we must firmly plant our decision-making feet, and not in the swampy quagmire of our subjective internal feelings.

The absence of subjective peace may be due to any number of things: The Holy Spirit, Satan, an angel, a demon, emotions, a hormonal imbalance, insomnia, medication, illness, occupational stress, an approaching deadline, nagging uncertainties, timidity, cowardice, a new challenge brought about by a personally stretching promotion, etc.

Garry Friesen insightfully expresses why it's unwise to rely on inward peace as a trustworthy compass for decision-making:

> I was once the best man for a friend who was getting married in North Dakota. In order to get to our position "backstage" without being seen, we had to crawl through the church baptistery. Doubling as the unofficial photographer, I took a picture of the groom as he crawled through the baptistry, then the camera focused on Mike as he sat by the entrance door biting his fingernails with the wide-eyed look of a condemned convict.
>
> The pose was made in jest. But suppose that he had looked up at me at that moment and said, "Garry, I've prayed a lot about marrying Chris. But right now I feel so unsettled inside, I think the Lord must be telling me not to go through with it." What should I have done? Should I have stopped the wedding? Isn't that what best men are for?
>
> Of course, he didn't say that. And I didn't stop the wedding. Nor would I have—not without a more legitimate reason. If all marriages were called off because of nervous grooms, there would be no weddings. Such "lack of peace" is normal when one faces a major new step in life.
>
> Some people experience a lack of peace because of immaturity. Decisions entail responsibilities and result in consequences. An immature person may be unwilling to accept new responsibilities. That individual may resist even making the decision. And he will experience considerable anxiety. The Holy Spirit saying "no" to a decision does not produce such turmoil; it is the result of simply facing a difficult decision. Such inner anxiety reveals the need for emotional growth; it is not specific guidance from God.[2]

Who hasn't experienced the phenomenon of post-decision regret? A godly man makes a careful and prayerful decision to accept a new job, in a superior position, with a better company. But after he hands his resignation to his boss, he's of course flooded with feelings of vacillating self-doubt.

When I was in college, I became romantically attached to a fine Christian lady who was still in high school. It became evident to me that this relationship had become too intense too early. A realistic wedding date would be a number of years away, and the present passion was far too strong. I 'd been very foolish. I started things too early and permitted things to go too fast. Helped by wise counsel, I made the painful decision to end the relationship. After I told her the sad news, I did not immediately feel *peace* about it. I wept all the way home, and was many times tempted to turn back and retract my words. For days, I was plagued with emotional *post-decision regret*. But on principle, I stayed the course, and eventually I was given the joy of a *settled conviction* that the Lord was pleased with my quest for prudence and purity.

Just a few weeks ago, we left our son on a college campus for freshman orientation exercises; years of prayerful and careful decision-making were sealed with finality. While driving back home to the Holland area, I can't say we were at perfect peace, without nagging thoughts of wondering if we'd done the right thing. We would've been foolish to turn around and plead with our son to return home because we just didn't "feel *peace* about it." The soul that lives in accordance with manly dominion will not permit itself to be tossed to and fro by every wind of emotional anxiety or internal misgiving. Christian, please note: Subjective *peace* is not necessarily the compass needle for life-directing decisions.

Living according to the compass needle of subjective *peace*, often translates into a formula for passive cowardice and retreating withdrawal. When I was ten-years-old, I was scheduled to participate in a Little League tryout on a Saturday morning. In previous years, my older brothers (then ages eleven and twelve), always went with me. That year, they were playing for the school team instead. For the first time, I had to go it alone. I still remember that Friday night writhing on my mother's bed, telling her how I didn't want to go "all by myself" the next morning. "If the big boys aren't going to be there this year, I'd just rather not play." Certainly, I didn't feel *peace* about it! My insides were churning. My eyes were tearing. If my parents would have allowed me to withdraw, I know I would have had great "peace" about it. Wisely, my parents made me go, "all by myself." By the end of the tryout, I was taking ground balls as the starting shortstop for my team! It was a great season.

When Alex thinks of talking to a brother at church about a problem he's seen in that man's teenage son, a big knot swells up in his stomach. When Alex thinks about *ignoring the problem*, the knot unties into a loose, *peaceful* sense of relaxation. But then he thinks of:

> **Luke 6:31** *And just as you want people to treat you, treat them in the same way.*

> **Proverbs 27:6** *Faithful are the wounds of a friend, But deceitful are the kisses of an enemy.*

> **James 4:17** *Therefore, to one who knows the right thing to do, and does not do it, to him it is sin.*

Alex knows what he must do, and regardless of the knot that tightens up inside again, he's "gotta do what he's gotta do."

Think of Jonah again. The word of the Lord came to him saying, "Arise, go to Nineveh the great city, and cry against it, for their wickedness has come up before Me" (1:1). Jonah had no internal *peace* about this. He detested that pagan city and its inhabitants. He recoiled from such an irksome errand. So Jonah withdrew from his duty, found that comfortable hammock in that Tarshish bound ship, went down below into the hold of the ship, laid down, and fell into a "sound sleep" (1:5). Though now Jonah's compass needle appears to be reading "at peace," his ship is heading in a completely wrong, God-defying direction. The word of God, and not the winds of feeling, must direct our decisions.

Consider our Blessed Lord Jesus in the Garden of Gethsemane. His Father too had assigned him to an irksome errand. He must go to the cross. In many ways, He subjectively recoiled from drinking the cup that had been assigned to Him to drink.

> **Mark 14:33-36a** *And He took with Him Peter and James and John, and began to be very distressed and troubled. 34 And He said to them, "<u>My soul is deeply grieved</u> to the point of death; remain here and keep watch." 35 And He went a little beyond them, and fell to the ground, and began to pray that if it were possible, the hour might pass Him by. 36a And He was saying, "Abba! Father! All things are possible for Thee; remove this cup from Me;*

> **Luke 22:44** *And being in agony He was praying very fervently; and His sweat became like drops of blood, falling down upon the ground.*

Nevertheless, His *subjective feelings* were not His compass, but rather his Father's Word and will:

> **Mark 14:36b** *". . . yet not what I will, but what Thou wilt."*

Here is our pattern. As with our beloved Savior and Master, *God's Word* and not *our peace of mind*, must reign as king in our hearts and in our decisions. Here's the formula for deep and enduring peace. Who isn't awed by the calm boldness in our Lord Jesus as he returned to his disciples, stared down the Sanhedrin soldiers, answered before Caiaphas' court, and stood on Pilate's porch? Here is the peace of God enjoyed by the obedient man who's prayerfully sought God's will to be done. The Spirit emboldened conscience and soul of such a man makes him bold as a lion (Proverbs 28:1).

Surely it's sometimes our experience that God gives us a bold sense of peace or confidence prior to the finalizing of a decision. The settled conviction of our knowing the right thing to do also comes home to our hearts in what might be identified as a subjective feeling of peace. Such enjoyable experiences are often the fruits of godly decision making, but not the root of it. We must build our decision-making processes not on the subjective and mystical quagmire of internal feelings, but on the objective and revelational rock of scriptural principle. We must make our decisions by thinking scripturally with our minds and not by feeling mystically with our emotions.

Don't permit yourself to be a pawn of your feelings and emotions. Don't be a four-ball! Exercise a manly dominion!

1 Geoffrey B. Wilson, *Philippians* (Edinburgh: Banner of Truth, 1983), p.94
2 *Decision Making and the Will of God*, p.143

Chapter 14
Wisdom #1

When I was in grade school, the blackboard was a standard feature in every classroom. At the end of each school day, the organized teacher would make sure that the blackboards were thoroughly erased of all chalk scribbling in order that he might start with a clean slate the next morning. In the previous three chapters, we've spent time erasing the blackboards of our minds. Pop perspectives and folk theology have scribbled down many faulty formulas for decision making. *Impressions*, *providence*, and *peace* have incorrectly been made into variables that dominate the decision-making formula, nurturing an unbiblical passivity. Having wiped the slate of this scribble, we're now ready to discuss some biblical principles for godly decision making.

These principles are in keeping with our image-bearing obligation to exercise *manly dominion* through *subduing* and *ruling*.

1. Enlist Your Mind

As mentioned earlier, the New Testament insists on our aggressively employing our *minds*: "Be transformed by the renewing of your *mind*" (Romans 12:2); "Be renewed in the spirit of your *mind*" (Ephesians 4:23); "gird your *minds* for action" (1 Peter 1:13).

Sarah sits with her mother in the parking lot of the bridal shop where she'll purchase her long awaited, one and only wedding dress. She prays with Mom, and then they walk together toward the boutique. Upon entering, Sarah notices the sun has just burst out from behind the clouds, beaming a ray through the window and directly onto a beautiful gown on display. At this point, she may be tempted to mystically and passively put her mind in neutral. Instead of critically analyzing such variables as the degree of neckline plunge, the amount of back exposed, the opinion of her mother, and the dollar figure on the price tag, Sarah could become convinced that the circumstantial sunbeam is the Lord's answer to her prayer.

Don't live like that, Sarah. You're acting like a passive-purple four-ball, being pushed around by an ambiguous circumstance. Enlist your *mind*! *Think* through this decision.

A God-fearing church was without a pastor for nearly two years. On two consecutive Sundays, a visiting pastor preached to the congregation with a power that gripped the hearts of the hearers. Stirred by the apparently clear direction of the Spirit among them, the pulpit committee moved quickly to extend a call to the gifted preacher. Because of their nearly unanimous sense of God's leading, they neglected a thorough background check on the man's character and graces. They failed to carefully examine whether or not he met the practical qualifications for pastor as listed in 1 Timothy 3 and Titus 1. They neglected to do their homework. They didn't *think*. Primarily on the strength of the Spirit's *felt presence* in the man's four sermons, he was overwhelmingly voted in as the new pastor. In a few months, however, the people realized they'd made a horrible mistake. This seemingly great preacher was not a great man, not God's man, as they'd intuitively felt he was. In fact, he was a very foolish man who ended up nearly destroying the church.

There's a tendency in all of us to abdicate our duty of engaging in rigorous *mental work*. We're tempted to abandon our normal thought processes when God desires us to bear the burden of carefully thinking through the implications of our decisions. The Lord does supernaturally guide and direct us, but this is primarily through the Holy Spirit's *renewing our minds* and casting illuminating light onto the written Scriptures.

Psalm 119:105 *Thy word is a lamp to my feet, And a light to my path.*

When faced with a decision, we're responsible to do the *mind work.* What are the options here? Can we innovatively create additional options? With each option, what are the pros and the cons? With each pro and con, what are the moral implications? What do the Scripture say to these things? What are the chief priorities?

I remember in my sophomore year of college when a professor presented this analytical and intellectual approach to living the Christian life according to the written pages of the ancient Book. Frankly, I was appalled. It seemed so clinical, so sterile, so carnal; and so unspiritual. Ah, but a ray of sunlight beaming onto a dress, a heart stirred to an emotional pitch by a dynamic speaker; now these felt much more sacred, much more mysterious—much more spiritual.

Sinclair Ferguson wisely handles this complaint:

> It may be said, by way of objection, that this tends to lock God up in the pages of a book, and deny us any direct access to him and his will for our lives. Naturally, unless we maintain a real spirit of dependence upon the ministry of the Spirit leading us into the true meaning and application of the Scripture, this may happen. But the abuse of a true principle is not really an argument against it. The principle itself must be allowed to stand. This is not to deny the need of supernatural aid to know the will of God. *On the contrary, this is exactly what is being affirmed!* But what we need supernatural help to do is to understand and apply our only rule of life, our only source of the knowledge of God and his will — the Holy Scriptures.
>
> Does this not deny the many mysterious elements that so many Christians have discovered in the way God has led them? Not necessarily! There are several things we should notice.
>
> There is much that is *mysterious* about the way God guides us. What is plain to him is frequently obscure to us. *But we are not called by God to make the mysterious, the unusual, and the inexplicable, the rule of our lives, but his word.*[1]

So whether we're a Sarah buying a wedding dress, or a congregation considering a new pastor, or a parent deliberating about giving the green light to a teenager's Friday night plans, we're obligated to enlist our *minds* by carefully and thoroughly *thinking* the matter through.

2. Search the Scriptures

> **2 Timothy 3:16-17** *All Scripture is inspired by God and profitable for teaching, for reproof, for correction, for training in righteousness; 17 that the man of God may be adequate, equipped for every good work.*

The inerrant, infallible, authoritative Word of God makes us adequate and equips us for every good work, including the making of wise decisions. Therefore, the Scriptures must be carefully studied if their light is to be cast onto the path we should choose. But let's make sure that we don't substitute a *careless mishandling* of the Bible for a *careful studying* of the Bible.

Imagine a man in the middle of a long, severe winter. This year he once again finds himself weary of these long stretches of cold, snowy, gray, overcast days. Emotionally downcast, he begins to become discontent with his living situation. He even hints to his less than enthused wife that they uproot and move to Florida. She knows he goes through this every February! Then one morning in his daily Bible reading, he stumbles across Acts 8:26, where an angel of the Lord reveals to Philip what God wants him to do: "*Arise and go south* to the road that descends from Jerusalem to Gaza." It's in particular those words "*Arise and go south,*" that subjectively warm his heart. "Could it be that God, here in the Scripture, is directing me to Florida?" He then goes to read his daily portion of the Old Testament and comes across 2 Samuel 7:3, where after David shares his desire to build a house for the Lord, Samuel replies: "Go, do all that is in your mind, for the Lord is with you."

Would it be wise for this man to conclude that the Scriptures have provided him clear guidance to do all that is in his mind by arising and going south? Certainly not! We must not use the Bible as if it were a mystical crystal ball. We must study the Word according to sound principles of interpretation, respecting the historical, logical, grammatical, and theological context of each passage we consider. Only then, can sober minded applications be prudently made.

John Newton, the eighteenth-century slave trader, then pastor and composer of *Amazing Grace*, wrote of his own experience in contemplating the reception of a ministerial call to the parish of Warwick. While meditating on Acts 18:10, Newton read how God encouraged Paul to labor on fearlessly in Corinth because "I have many people in this city." John Newton initially thought that God was promising *him* great numerical success in Warwick.

> I remember, in going to undertake the care of a congregation, I was reading, as I walked in a green lane, "Fear not, Paul, I have much people in this city." But I soon afterwards was disappointed to find that Paul was not John, and that Corinth was not Warwick.[2]

John Newton also wrote insightfully on Divine Guidance:

> Others, when in doubt, have *opened the Bible at a venture*, and expected to find something to direct them in the first verse they should cast their eye upon. . . . if people will be governed by the occurrence of a single text of Scripture, without regarding the context, or duly comparing it with the general tenor of the word of God, and with their own circumstances, they may commit the greatest extravagances, expect the greatest impossibilities, and contradict the plainest dictates of common sense, while they think they have the word of God on their side. . . It is certain that matters big with important consequences have been engaged in, and the most sanguine (upbeat) expectations formed, upon no better warrant than dipping (as it is called) upon a text of Scripture."[3]

How then should a man search the Scriptures to find light and guidance from God's Word? He should look for, not a personalized whisper, but rather, for overarching principles that apply to his case. For example, he has fifteen years of seniority with his prosperous employer, but presently has no job prospects in Florida. Can a man with four children justify such an abrupt move? Certainly, financial stability is a crucial biblical priority that must be considered.

> **1 Timothy 5:8** *But if anyone does not provide for his own, and especially for those of his household, he has denied the faith, and is worse than an unbeliever.*

His two oldest children presently attend a fine high school with excellent teachers and quality friends. His son is now a junior and is the point guard on the basketball team. Is the timing of a Florida move prudent?

›lossians 3:21 *Fathers, do not exasperate your children, that they may not lose heart.*

His wife is strongly opposed to uprooting at this season of life.

1 Peter 3:7 *You husbands likewise, live with your wives in an understanding way, as with a weaker vessel, since she is a woman; and grant her honor as a fellow heir of the grace of life, so that your prayers may not be hindered.*

He presently attends a solid, biblical church, but is very unsure of what's available in the Florida communities to which he's pondered moving.

Proverbs 4:23 *Watch over your heart with all diligence, For from it flow the springs of life.*

Matthew 6:33 *"But seek first His kingdom and His righteousness;*

Both sets of grandparents live in Michigan.

Proverbs 17:6 *Grandchildren are the crown of old men, And the glory of sons is their fathers.*

The Balmy breezes of March are just around the corner.

Proverbs 13:12 *Hope deferred makes the heart sick, But desire fulfilled is a tree of life.*

After conscientiously and prudently searching the Scripture, a man may become convinced that the biblical priorities weigh more heavily on the side of his enduring through shivering and depressing winters, than his personally enjoying the year round warmth and comfort of the Sunshine State!

Understand that for some decisions, searching Scripture can be a long and laborious process; while for other decisions, the process may be relatively swift and immediate. Just as a musically well-trained ear can almost immediately distinguish a good musician from a bad one, so too a biblically well-trained soul can almost immediately distinguish a good decision from a bad one.

John Newton helpfully summarizes the issues:

> But how then may the Lord's guidance be expected? . . . In general, he guides and directs his people, by affording them, in answer to prayer, the light of his Holy Spirit, which enables them to understand and to love the Scriptures. The word of God is not to be used as a lottery; nor is it designed to instruct us by shreds and scraps, which detached from their proper places, have no determinate import; but it is to furnish us with just principles, right apprehensions to regulate our judgments and affections, and thereby to influence and direct our conduct.
>
> They who study the Scriptures, in an humble dependence upon divine teaching, are convinced of their own weakness, are taught to make a true estimate of everything around them, are gradually formed into a spirit of submission to the will of God, discover the nature and duties of their several situations and relations in life, and the snares and temptations to which they are exposed. The word of God which dwells richly in them, is a preservative from error, light to their feet, and a spring of strength and consolation.
>
> By treasuring up the doctrines, precepts, promises, examples, and exhortations of Scripture, in their *minds*, and daily comparing themselves with the rule by which they walk, they grow into an habitual frame of spiritual wisdom, and acquire a gracious *taste*, which enables them to judge of right and wrong with a degree of readiness and certainty, as a *musical ear* judges of sounds. And they are seldom mistaken, because they are influenced by the love of Christ, which rules in their hearts, and a regard to the glory of God, which is the great object they have in view.[4]

In this way, we are kept from being pushed around purple-four-ball-like by every thrust and bumper of emotion, fancy and circumstance.

> **Psalm 119:99** *I have more insight than all my teachers, For Thy testimonies are my meditation.*

3. Seek Counsel

Emma was attending college to acquire a B.S. in nursing. During the first year, she was able to commute with the family's extra car, but when she picked up a part-time position at the hospital, and her sister driving, it was clear to Emma that the time had come for her purchase her own car. She wisely shopped around, comparing price, mileage, and appearance factors. Finally, she found a beautiful silver import. The price seemed very reasonable. She fell in love with it. She prayed about it. She bought it. Three weeks later, upon hearing strange noises from under the hood, she visited a mechanic, who informed her that the engine needed to be rebuilt. He also said that this model is notorious for this problem, and that the necessary new parts would be very expensive since they were made overseas. Emma ended up paying for another half of a car.

Jerry was soon to begin college and needed a car. He'd been searching the papers for months, getting a feel for the market. Finally, he began viewing and test-driving the possibilities. One afternoon, he drove a sporty Pontiac up the driveway, and announced to his Dad that he had a "pretty good one" out front. When his Dad walked out of the garage, he passed by the brown van which Grandpa had endorsed before Dad had bought it a few years earlier. Dad climbed into the Grand Am with Jerry and headed for the garage of Tom the mechanic, who said, "I'd never buy a four cylinder of this particular model. Sixes are fine, but the fours are trouble."

For Jerry, the break up was painful, but a few days later, the berry colored Chevy made him forget all about the Pontiac beauty. After looking it over, Dad recommended he have Tom take a look at it too. With a bit of emotional reluctance, Jerry took it to Tom who checked the radiator and found oil mixed in with the water. The head gasket needed to be replaced. The estimated repair cost was nearly $1000. The man selling the Monte agreed to make the repairs and sell it at the same previously negotiated price. The seeking of wise counsel enabled Jerry to dodge the bullet that hit Emma.

Moses took advice from his gentile father-in-law, Jethro, who recommended he delegate the judging of civil cases to trained and able men who could ease Moses' workload.

> **Exodus 18:18-19** *"You will surely wear out, both yourself and these people who are with you, for the task is too heavy for you; you cannot do it alone. 19 "Now listen to me: I shall give you counsel, and God be with you…*

David took the contrary advice of Abigail when he'd decided to slaughter every male in Nabal's house (1 Samuel 25:23ff). Rehoboam foolishly chose to disregard the counsel of his gray-headed advisers and ended up splitting the kingdom by his youthful impetuosity (1 Kings 12:1ff).

Manly dominion and aggressiveness does not independently plow forward without seeking wise advice. The man of true dominion is able to rule and subdue his pride that boasts in his own competence. He's able to *rule and subdue* his emotions, which at times *fall in love* with an option that may be jeopardized by contrary counsel. He's able to *rule and subdue* his mind so that he's not passively pushed around to and fro by every word of advice he receives from various quarters. The man of biblical dominion will carefully evaluate his sought-out advice, and factor it all into his decision-making formula.

> **Proverbs 11:14** *Where there is no guidance, the people fall, But in abundance of counselors there is victory.*

> **Proverbs 12:15** *The way of a fool is right in his own eyes, But a wise man is he who listens to counsel.*

> **Proverbs 13:10** *Through presumption comes nothing but strife, But with those who receive counsel is wisdom.*

> **Proverbs 15:22** *Without consultation, plans are frustrated, But with many counselors they succeed.*

> **Proverbs 20:18** *Prepare plans by consultation, And make war by wise guidance.*

George Lawson comments on these proverbial principles:

> In our private concerns it is dangerous to trust our own wisdom, and it is in our interest to advise with wise and faithful friends, in every important business of life...The greatest fools are those who have the highest opinion of their own wisdom. Their self-esteem disposes them to neglect the advice of others, and to prosecute their own schemes, however foolish and dangerous, till they meet with fatal disappointments, which, after all, can hardly open their eyes, clean shut with pride and vanity. The wisest men are they who are most sensible of their need to avail themselves of the wisdom of others, and most qualified to make a proper use of counsel.[5]

Ben had become romantically attached to a beautiful young lady. The radiance of her lovely face and form melted him into a puddle of infatuation. All he could see in her were good things. He was "blinded by the light." He couldn't (or wouldn't) see her subtle deceitfulness, her lack of spirituality, and her selfishness. Thankfully, some loving friends came alongside Ben and faithfully showed him the bigger picture.

> **Proverbs 31:30** *Charm is deceitful and beauty is vain, But a woman who fears the LORD, she shall be praised.*

The Word of God is our chief counselor. The Scriptures are our ultimate spectacles. But sometimes they get fogged up, and so we need to rely heavily on the counsel of trustworthy advisers such as parents, pastors, and seasoned saints.

14 / WISDOM, 1

1 *Discovering God's Will*, p. 32

2 John Newton, *Out of the Depths* (Chicago: Moody Press; first published, 1764), p. 155

3 *Letters of John Newton* (Banner of Truth, 1988), pp.78-79

4 Ibid., pp. 81-82

5 George Lawson, *Commentary on Proverbs* (Grand Rapids: Kregel Publications, 1993), pp. 136; 158-9.

Chapter 15
Wisdom #2

4. Pray Earnestly

A few years ago I was scheduled to preach in a Suburb of Toledo, Ohio. While my host was driving me to the church building, I observed the steep grade and depth of the ditches on each side of the nearly shoulder less country road on which we were speeding. "Look at those ditches," I blurted. "We're driving on a tightrope! Forget the eye contact with me. Keep your eyes on the road!"

So it is also with the narrow road of the Christian life. There's always a dangerous ditch on the right or left. Regarding manly dominion in general, on the left is the ditch of "passive abdicating"; and on the right is the ditch of "atheistic enterprising." Regarding decision making in particular, on the left is the ditch of "mystical presumption"; and on the right is the ditch of "humanistic deliberation." Both ditches are deadly and must be avoided.

In godly decision making, we must employ our minds, search the Scriptures and seek counsel. But the process is not merely a cerebral endeavor. It's an altogether *sacred* and *spiritual* exercise. We're foolish sinners in need of God's wisdom. Yes, we have the Scriptures, but without the illumination of the Spirit, we're blind as bats. Without His help, we won't see the principles clearly, and so we'll misapply them badly.

That's why James writes:

> James 1:5 *But if any of you lacks wisdom, let him ask of God, who gives to all men generously and without reproach, and it will be given to him.*

The most brilliantly conceived plans and decisions, prayerlessly executed, are more often than not doomed to failure. Joshua chose competent warriors and implemented a shrewd battle plan against

Amalek, but only when Moses' hands were upraised heavenward on the hill, did Joshua prevail in the battle (Exodus 17:8-13).

Yes, we must think through options, survey the Bible, collate advice, and hammer out a decision. But,

> **Psalm 127:1-2** *Unless the LORD builds the house, They labor in vain who build it; Unless the LORD guards the city, The watchman keeps awake in vain. 2 It is vain for you to rise up early, To retire late, To eat the bread of painful labors; For He gives to His beloved even in his sleep.*

Think of Eleazar, the servant of Abraham who was commissioned by his master to find and decide on a bride for his son Isaac. He saturated the whole process in prayer:

> **Genesis 24:12** *And he said, "O LORD, the God of my master Abraham, please grant me success today, and show lovingkindness to my master Abraham."*

The very first soul he met at the well was Rebekah, the daughter of Bethuel, son of Milcah, wife of Abraham's brother Nahor! Such are the blessed benefits of prayer in decision making. So often *we have not because we've asked not* (James 4:2).

Rick, a man in our church, is a reservist in the Army National Guard. It's December of 2002 and he's been presented with the making of a monumental decision. United Nations inspectors are searching for weapons of mass destruction in Iraq, and President Bush is pessimistic about Saddam's submission. War may be imminent. The four hundred men of Rick's tank battalion have been asked to volunteer for a year mission of guard duty on Michigan military bases. The needed two hundred guard-duty soldiers will have to take full-year furloughs from their civilian jobs, but will be able to commute and stay home for three full days per week. The two hundred men who don't volunteer for the guard duty may be able to spend a peaceful year advancing in their civilian jobs, but run the risk of being shipped out of state or even off to combat in Iraq, if war breaks out.

What's Rick to do? What's best for his soul, his three children, his country, his civilian career, and for his five-month pregnant wife? Such a man must lay out a flow chart of all the priorities and potential risks. But when all this *calculating* has been done, who knows what a day may bring forth (Proverbs 27:1)? Only the Lord does! Here's where a man is thrust to his knees before the Throne of Grace in prayer. "Oh my Father, I can't see a second beyond this moment. Please guide me in the way I should go!"

> Beloved! You know that many times a favourite at court gets more through one secret appeal, by one private request to his prince, than a tradesman or a merchant gets in twenty years' labour and pains, etc. So a Christian many times gets more by one secret appeal, by one private request to the King of kings, than many others do by trading long in the more public (and *calculating*) duties of religion.[1]

So in our dominion-minded decision making, let's give ourselves to prayer. Not just to halfhearted token prayer, but to full-hearted, earnest prayer.

> **James 5:16b-18** *The effective prayer of a righteous man can accomplish much. 17 Elijah was a man with a nature like ours, and he prayed earnestly that it might not rain; and it did not rain on the earth for three years and six months. 18 And he prayed again, and the sky poured rain, and the earth produced its fruit.*

> Some mercies are not given to us except in an answer to importunate prayer. There are blessings which, like ripe fruit, drop into your hand the moment you touch the branch. But there are others which require you to shake the tree again and again, until you make it rock with its vehemence of your exercise, for only then will the fruit fall down.[2]

So in our prayer closets we've got to get down to business. We must employ manly dominion by subduing and ruling over carnal distractions, fleshly aversions, and worldly interruptions. Prayer empowers our endeavors.

5. Make a Decision

During my senior year in college, Dianne became much more than a friend to me. After the graduation ceremony, I untied my golden honors cords that I had worn with my gown, handed one of them to Dianne, and said, "I'm hoping that maybe someday we'll be able to tie these back together again." I thought I was so dashing and romantic!

She returned to Iowa for the summer. The mailman complained during those months that her weekly perfume-scented letters to me made his jeep smell like a boutique.

She returned back to Michigan in August where we resumed our courtship. She was the "woman who feared the Lord" I'd been longing for. Yes, I was thinking about deciding to ask her to marry me. Yes, I was praying about it. Yes, I was working on it. But then one day in late November my Dad took me aside and said, "If you haven't asked her by Christmas, just forget it!" He was right! What was I waiting for? I was just procrastinating. Scriptural principles, providence, counsel, and conviction had converged. By Christmas, we were engaged.

Enlisting our minds, searching the Scriptures, seeking counsel, and praying fervently are all crucial in decision-making groundwork. But at the end of the day, you've got to make a decision, and this typically takes *decisiveness* and *courage*. Procrastination and postponement are often displays not of prudence, but of cowardice and passivity. Here again, we need to aggressively exercise manly dominion by *subduing* our fear and sloth. We need to *rule*.

Surely, there's no virtue in making snap decisions.

> **Proverbs 19:2** *Also it is not good for a person to be without knowledge,*
> *And he who makes haste with his feet errs.*

I think this characteristic of "holy pause" is one of the general traits implanted by the Lord in males making them well suited for headship in the family and church. Women generally seem to be more intuitive. They seem to come to conclusions more quickly. Men, on the other hand, generally want to take more time to try to wrap their brains around the issue. Though at times this slower process may make us appear dull-headed and overly cautious to our wives, in the long run it's a prudent approach.

But our strength can become our weakness. A chronic and unhealthy putting off of decisions can plague us. This passive-purple-four-ballism can bring great frustration to a wife who's trying to administer a godly household.

"Honey, I've been asking you since May about how we're going to educate the two youngest children this year. You've made it clear that public school is out, but what's it going to be: homeschool or Christian school? It's already July, and we've got to make a decision!"

It's time to play the man. It's time to face the twin lions of *indecisiveness* and *procrastination*. It's time to subdue those prowling hesitations by putting them under your feet. Make the decision. Be decisive. Be a man.

John Murray gives a helpful analysis of the Holy Spirit's assistance in drawing us to holy conclusions in finalizing the decision-making process:

> The demands of God's Word are all-pervasive, and the revelation God has given to us of his will in the Scriptures applies to us in every situation. It is equally necessary to remember that we must rely upon the Holy Spirit to direct and guide us in the understanding and application of God's will as revealed in the Scripture, and we must be constantly conscious of our need of the Holy Spirit to apply the Word effectively to us in every situation. The function of the Holy Spirit in such matters is that of *illumination* as to what the will of the Lord is, and of imparting to us the *willingness* and *strength* to do that will.
>
> It needs also to be recognized that, as we are the subjects of this illumination and are responsive to it, and as the Holy Spirit is operative in us to the doing of God's will, we shall have feelings, impressions, convictions, urges, inhibitions, impulses, burdens, resolutions. Illumination and direction by the Spirit through the Word of God will focus themselves in our consciousness in these ways. We are not automata (robots). And we are finite. We must not think, therefore, that a strong or overwhelming feeling or impression or conviction, which we may not be able at a particular time to explain to others, or ourselves is necessarily *irrational* or *fanatically mystical* (direct revelation from God). Since we are human and finite and not always able to view all the factors or considerations in their relations to one another, the sum total of these factors and considerations bearing upon a particular situation may focus themselves in our consciousness in what we may describe as a strong feeling or impression. In many cases such a feeling or impression is *highly rational* and is the only way in which our consciousness, at a particular juncture, can take in or react to a complex manifold of thoroughly proper considerations. In certain instances it may take us a long time to understand the meaning or implications of that impression.[3]

A mindset of manly dominion will rise to the occasion by setting and facing prudent deadlines and boldly making decisions.

Ken and his wife Anita, both Canadian citizens, were in Michigan for an extended weekend as Ken had just accepted a position as an engineer with a local pharmaceutical company. The weekend was dedicated to house hunting. After viewing over 30 houses, Ken sensed that Anita was feeling the stress of finding a suitable nest for their three young boys. On the last day, allowing Anita to sleep in, Ken rose early in the morning to spy out a "For Sale By Owner" home he'd seen from the street while out with a realtor. Though it was early, the homeowner gladly gave Ken a tour.

As Ken analyzed the design, floor plan, square footage, surroundings, quality, decorating, and price of the home, it was clear to him that this address was exactly what they were looking for. Ken quickly called Anita and soon they were both touring the home. This was clearly an exceptional buy. All the key priorities were present. Then the homeowner mentioned, "Another couple is due to take a tour within the hour." Not wanting to miss this exceptional opportunity, or to get into a bidding contest, Ken made an offer right there on the spot. The owner accepted it. Then Ken asked if the seller had any paperwork to sign. Bewildered, the owner confessed he didn't know how to prepare a buy/sell agreement. Ken replied, "Where's your computer?" Just as the other interested couple was driving over, Ken and his bride were driving away with a signed contract for their dream house. Ken got the kisses. He gave God the glory.

Ken acted like a man. Though the stakes were high, he rose to the occasion, and acted decisively in securing an abode for his family. In a world where it's often, "You snooze, you lose," Ken subdued and ruled. Like Nehemiah standing before King Artaxerxes, when given an unexpected opportunity to journey to and rebuild Jerusalem, he decisively accepted on the spot. "So it pleased the king to send me, and I gave him a definite time" (Nehemiah 2:6b).

In contrast is Jim Elliot's courtship of his wife, Elisabeth. In Elisabeth's book, *Passion and Purity*, she chronicles her over-six-year courtship with Jim. She escorts the reader through the twists and turns of Jim's method of seeking God's will for his life. Sometimes, Jim said the light was *red*. At other times, he said it was *yellow*. Occasionally, it was *almost green*. Although he loved his future wife dearly, he didn't give her a clear indication of his intentions. But his explanation to Elisabeth was Isaiah 59:9: "We look for light but all is darkness, for light of dawn, but we walk in gloom."

It was Jim's mother, however, who accurately cut to the quick. Elisabeth narrates:

> His mother wrote in August to invite me to stop in Portland on my way home from Alberta. . . . It was the annual Labor Day conference, and the Elliot men were very much in view on the platform as speakers, at the back managing things, milling around as hosts. We had little time for talk until it was over, when we went to Mount Tabor Park. We sat on the grass. *Here it comes*, I thought. But again it was Isaiah 59:9. Still looking for light. Still no word as to whether God might have "changed His mind." Why should I have entertained such a foolish hope? Well, because I couldn't help hoping against hope.
>
> I helped Jim's mother with the laundry one morning, and as she was hauling the sheets out of the machine she suddenly said, "I know these Elliot men. They can never make up their minds. If I were you I'd tell Jim it's now or never."[4]

Don't be paralyzed into passivity by the fear of making a decision. Don't be a four-ball. Be a cue-stick-carrying man of dominion. Analyze the table, and within a responsible period of time, take your shot.

6. Carry It Through

If you've enlisted your mind, searched the Scriptures, sought counsel, prayed fervently, and made a decision, don't allow minor obstacles to derail it. Internal doubts or circumstantial impediments should not be interpreted as God's now flashing a *yellow* or a *red light*.

After spending years in the decision-making process, Jerry decided to pursue engineering at a highly regarded technical school. During the first week, he heard students' talk of how difficult the engineering program was. He was told that almost half of them *change majors* after the first year. He heard that Calculus was a "weed-em-out" course. He heard from an alumnus how he'd begun his freshman year with approximately 300 prospective engineers. Four years later, only 60 graduated with an engineering degree. Then in the third month, Jerry hit stormy seas in Calculus. He'd never been academically tossed about like this before. It was taking all he had to keep himself from capsizing. He began to think, "Maybe I made a wrong decision here. Maybe it's not God's will for me to press on in this engineering course." He became seasick with *post-decision regret.* He was tempted to *change majors* right then and there.

Was God telling Jerry to quit engineering? Maybe. But maybe not! A change of course is not necessarily God's will simply because we encounter *obstacles* and *misgivings.* During Paul's second missionary journey, he had a vision of a man from Macedonia appealing to him, saying "Come over to Macedonia and help us" (Acts 16:9). He arrives at Philippi and ends up getting beaten with rods and thrown into prison (Acts 16:16-40). He moves further into Macedonia where a riotous mob drives him out of town (Acts 17:1-9). But Paul didn't interpret *adverse providences* as *red lights* from God.

> **1 Corinthians 16:8-9** *But I shall remain in Ephesus until Pentecost; 9 for a wide door for effective service has opened to me, and there are many adversaries.*

Elsewhere, he writes:

> **2 Corinthians 7:5** *For even when we came into Macedonia our flesh had no rest, but we were afflicted on every side: conflicts without, fears within.*

Adversities and misgivings didn't cause him to change his course. In each case, Paul had decided on a plan, and he labored to carry it through.

In the case of Jerry, an older man told him that studying to become an engineer was like training to become a Navy Seal; only the ones who resolve stick it out through extreme adversity make it. Sure, they hate bobbing up and down in ten feet of water while their ankles and wrists are tied behind their backs. Sure, they hate standing at attention for hours half naked, soaking wet on a beach in a driving 40-degree wind. But those who stick it out, become highly esteemed and privileged Seals. Sure, you hate the irksome problems of calculus, but if you stick it out, you can become an *engineer.* On Jerry's next calculus test he scored 95%.

Think again of Nehemiah. He'd made a decision to leave Artaxerxes' Persian palace and journey to Jerusalem where his plan to rebuild the walls would be implemented. But upon arriving, he discovered that the rubble was far more extensive than he thought (2:12-17a). He faced an unexpected military threat from Sanballat, Tobiah, & Company (4:7-8). He was harassed by usurious financial bullying from the nobles (5:1-13); and became the target of an elaborate assassination plot (6:1-14). But even these major obstacles didn't cause him to *derail his decision* to rebuild Jerusalem.

> **Nehemiah 6:15-16** *So the wall was completed on the twenty-fifth of the month Elul, in fifty-two days. 16 And it came about when all our enemies heard of it, and all the nations surrounding us saw it, they lost their confidence; for they recognized that this work had been accomplished with the help of our God.*

What pastor hasn't had the experience of deciding on a passage on which he should preach on the Lord's Day, carefully and prayerfully preparing the sermon, but not sleeping well the night before due to internal misgivings about the sermon's content? He awakens and wonders if he should abandon the ship of that sermon. He thinks, "No, I made a careful and prayerful decision, and I'll stick with it." He preaches the sermon and enjoys the wind of heaven in his sails.

Misgivings and post decision regret are no reason to derail a prudently made decision. Being tossed to and fro by every wind of providence and wave of feeling is no way to *subdue* and *rule* the ship of your life.

I once typed out an email to a fellow pastor. In it, I pressed his conscience on an important matter. When I pushed the "send" button, I encountered a software malfunction. This had never happened to me before. Considering the delicate content of the letter, I wondered if the Lord was blocking my way just as the donkey blocked Balaam's way. I pondered and prayed, but was still convinced of the appropriateness of the letter's content. Six more times I tried to send it, but each time there was a problem. "Surely I must be kicking against the goads," I thought. "But then again, Satan may be hindering me." After another prayerful re-evaluation, I decided that the conviction of my conscience compelled me to send those words, and if I need to rewrite them in crayon and send them by homing pigeon, so help me God, I'll send this note to my friend. On the eighth attempt to *send* the email, I was successful.

Once a man of dominion has carefully and prayerfully made a decision, unless *cogent* information or convincing circumstances arise to *compel* a retraction or revision, he'll enlist every lawful and prudent means available to him, to *carry it through.*

He'll refuse to play the four-ball.

Manly Dominion in Spiritual Living

Principles of Manly Dominion and aggressive subduing provide a man with an effective recipe for great achievement.

> **Proverbs 12:24** *The hand of the diligent will rule.*

The diligent and aggressive hand of Bill Gates rules in the field of business. The diligent and aggressive hand of Michael Jordan has ruled in the field of professional basketball. The diligent and aggressive hand of Stephen Spielberg rules in the field of entertainment. Their assertive plowing in their respective fields has produced admirable success.

But worldly success alone is appallingly hollow.

> **Matthew 16:26** "*For what will a man be profited, if he gains the whole world, and forfeits his soul? Or what will a man give in exchange for his soul?...*"

> **1 Timothy 4:7b-8** *discipline yourself for the purpose of godliness; 8 for bodily discipline is only of little profit, but godliness is profitable for all things, since it holds promise for the present life and also for the life to come.*

Man's primary mandate from God is success not in the *material realm* alone, but in the *spiritual realm* primarily. The pursuit of godliness is our ultimate errand. The dominion principles of subduing and ruling must be chiefly employed toward the glorification of our Maker, and the salvation of our souls.

The Westminster Shorter Catechism addresses this in its first question:

> Q. What is man's chief end?
> *A. Man's chief end is to glorify God and to enjoy Him forever.*

We now, therefore, want to turn a corner and focus our attention on some fields of endeavor that relate directly to the realm of *spiritual living*. Most importantly in these fields, we must labor to drive out the plague of passive-purple four-ballism, and implement the principles of manly dominion.

1 *Works of Thomas Brooks, Vol.2* (Edinburgh: Banner of Truth, 1861-67; reprinted, 1980), pp.183-84
2 Charles Haddon Spurgeon, *The Metropolitan Tabernacle Pulpit, Vol.21* (Pasadena, TX: Pilgrim Publications, 1920), p.437
3 *Collected Writings of John Murray, Vol.1, "The Guidance of the Holy Spirit"* (Edinburgh: Banner of Truth, 1976), pp.187-188
4 *Passion and Purity*, pp.139-140

Chapter 16
Manly Dominion in Spiritual Living: Personal Devotions

A couple of years ago, my wife decided that we'd have a vegetable garden. Norm, our neighborhood gardening expert, showed up one Saturday with his rototiller, ready to dig in. When he saw the size of the parcel we'd staked out, he scratched his head and asked Dianne if she was sure she wanted such a big plot. Full of spring enthusiasm, my wife gave Norm the green light, and before long all the rows were planted. Now all we had to do was wait for the bumper crop!

But it didn't work that way. Dianne encountered that summer *The Law of the Wilderness.* The wilderness aggressively resists man's attempts to *subdue* it. She discovered that his orderly rows were almost immediately assaulted by strangling legions of thorns and thistles and weeds of every imaginable variety. Dianne, assisted valiantly by our second son, Calvin, was engaged in a serious battle. If she neglected the garden for two or three days, she was faced with hordes of barbarian intruders. Upon returning from a late July to early August vacation, the plot had been almost irreparably ransacked. Her garden had become a forest of weeds. A bumper crop it wasn't.

This is the way it is with keeping the heart. If we don't exercise the manly dominion principles of subduing and ruling, our hearts will succumb to the *Law of the Wilderness.* They'll be strangled by the cares and concerns of the world (Mk. 4:19). They'll be overrun by the aggressive and noxious weeds of the flesh (Gal. 5:17). They'll be ransacked by the Devil who loves to sow choking tares in with the wheat (Mt. 13:24-26).

Solomon wisely commissions us to take up the chronic task of keeping our hearts:

> **Proverbs 4:23** *Watch over your heart with all diligence, For from it flow the springs of life.*

Solomon enlists here the imagery of an ancient well. In ancient Palestine, survival depended on access to water. The hot and dry climate required that enterprising methods be used to get it. Men would dig deep shafts or cisterns to tap the subterranean waters that sustained life to their families, flocks, and crops. A man's well was the source of life for his entire estate. If the well dries up, famine follows.

Solomon is saying that a man's heart is the wellspring for his entire life; its health, its relationships, its endeavors. The Lord, through His Spirit, makes flow the subterranean waters (*a river of living waters*, John 7:37-38). The man, through his religious exercises, accesses the bucketfuls of refreshing fluid.

Solomon says, "watch over" or "guard" your heart. Ancient wells weren't like our modern faucets that need no maintenance, and gush at the turning of a knob. An ancient well was vulnerable to being plugged up by blowing sand and debris, being *putrefied* by an animal's falling in and dying, or being sabotaged by an enemy. Because of these very real threats, a man needed to jealously and conscientiously maintain and protect his well. So too, a Christian must "guard" his heart "with all diligence."

Genesis 26:12-22 narrates Isaac's chronic problems with his wells being plugged up and disputed over by the Philistines. John Owen wrote a classic treatise called *The Nature, Power, Deceit, and Prevalency of the Remainders of Indwelling Sin in Believers Together with the Ways of Its Working and Means of Prevention.* In it he refers to Isaac's Philistine problem in keeping his wells, and applies it to the Christian's indwelling sin problem in keeping his heart.

> Isaac digged wells, but the Philistines stopped them up, and his flocks had no benefit by them.... If care be not taken, if diligence and watchfulness be not used, and all means that are appointed by God to keep a quick and living sense of spiritual thoughts upon the soul, they will dry

> up and decay; and, consequently, that obedience that should spring from them will do so also. . . . Now, while these and the like springs are kept open in the souls of converted sinners, they constrain them to a vigorous, active holiness. They can never do enough for God.[1]

As a Christian, my heart is a well. The land of my Christian life is teeming with hostile forces determined to do me harm by separating me from my water source. The world hourly blows in the burying sands of vanity. My flesh (indwelling sin) welcomes in unclean sights and sounds that putrefy the waters. The Devil works hard with distractions to harass and dispute my every attempt drink deeply.

My heart will be kept open, fresh, and clear only by my aggressively "watching," "guarding," and "keeping" the condition of my heart. Passive negligence in my devotional life will result in certain famine. So when I wake up in the morning, I need to have a manly dominion mindset that resolves to rule and subdue over my heart. If I go to my prayer/Bible reading closet, and discover that my heart is stopped up with apathy and carnality, I shouldn't be surprised, deflated, or crestfallen. I should understand that my heart is disputed territory, and that it will be kept in a healthy condition only by hard work. When I find my heart stopped up, it's not time to turn away from the closet with a bone-dry bucket. It's time for me to roll up my sleeves and get to work. It's time to do some holy *digging* by resolute prayer, attentive reading, and purposeful meditation.

A friend of mine, Kevin, resolves not to leave his closet in the morning until he gets at least one heart-gripping contemplation that he daily jots down in his Franklin Planner. He won't leave his well until he gets at least a jug full of refreshment for his day's work in the field of his corporate vocation.

We need to rid ourselves of that romantic idealism that thinks our regenerated hearts will, like a faucet, gush at the turning of a knob. That's not what the Bible advertises. We must not say with fainting dejection, "I must be missing something," simply because we're habitually required to work at keeping our hearts in a good condition.

A spiritually weary man in Minnesota said to me, "It seems like such a tedious chore to keep my heart in a good condition." He probably thought I'd be surprised at his confession. I wasn't. I told him that I too had to dig hard to keep my heart open. His eyes were brightened by the revelation that no temptation had overtaken him but such as is common to man (1 Corinthians 10:13). Heart keeping is a standard daily chore of every Christian.

Sure, the Lord is the ultimate Keeper of our hearts. He makes sure that the internal soul rivers of Living Water do not dry up. But He enlists our hands and fingers.

Charles Bridges wisely comments on Proverbs 4:23:

> Then when I know my heart, and feel it to be so dangerous, and in such dangers, the question forces itself upon me: "Can I keep my [own] heart?" Certainly not. But, though it be God's work, it is man's agency. Our efforts are his instrumentality. He implants an active principle, and sustains the unceasing exercise (Phil. 2:12-13; Jude 24 with 21). [2]

Consider J. C. Ryle's workman-like advice as it relates to a Christian's common discouragement as it relates to daily Bible reading:

> This paper may fall into the hands of someone who reads the Bible much, and yet fancies he is no better for his reading. This is a crafty temptation of the devil. At one stage he says, "Do not read the Bible at all." At another he says, "Your reading does you no good; give it up." Are you that man? I feel for you from the bottom of my soul. Let me try to do you good.
>
> Do you think you are getting no good from the Bible, merely because you do not see that good day by day? The greatest effects are by no means those which make the most noise, and are most easily observed. The greatest effects are often silent, quiet, and hard to detect at the time they are being produced. Think of the influence of the moon upon the earth, and the air upon the human lungs. Remember how silently the dew falls, and how imperceptibly the grass grows. There may be far more doing than you think in your soul by your Bible reading.
>
> The Word may be gradually producing deep impressions on your heart, of which you are not at present aware. . . . Settle it down in your mind as an established rule, that, whether you feel it at the moment or not, you are inhaling spiritual health by reading the Bible, and insensibly becoming more strong[3].

Again, Ryle offers us help regarding our common struggles in *private prayer.*

> If I know anything of a Christian's heart, you to whom I now speak are often sick of your own prayers. You never enter into the Apostle's words, "When I would do good, evil is present with me" (Rom. 7:21), so thoroughly as you sometimes do upon your knees. You can understand David's words, "I hate vain thoughts." You can sympathize with that poor converted Hottentot, who was overheard praying, "Lord, deliver me from all my enemies; and above all, from that bad man myself!" There are few children of God who do not often find the season of prayer a season of conflict. The devil has special wrath against us when he sees us on our knees. Yet I believe that prayers which *cost us no trouble* should be regarded with great suspicion. I believe we are very poor judges of the goodness of our prayers, and that the prayer which pleases us least, often pleases God the most.[4]

Finally, it's essential that we premeditatedly commit ourselves to daily heart work. We've got to carve it into our schedules as a priority and not leave it to "whenever I get around to it," or "whenever the right circumstances arise." This is a formula for spiritual famine.

David commits himself with holy resolution:

> **Psalm 5:3** *<u>In the morning</u>, O LORD, <u>Thou wilt</u> hear my voice; In the morning <u>I will</u> order my prayer to Thee and eagerly watch.*

Amber is the mother of three very young boys. She resolved to make devotional heart work a priority. She set the early morning as the time. Her boys had other ideas. When they heard her moving about the house in the early morning, they'd wake up and sabotage her closet time. Instead of being harassed by untimely behavior, she drew a line in the sand. "You boys don't get out of bed until 8:00 am." This would give her time to shower, groom, read, and pray before her horses were let loose. Stuart, her three year-old, pleaded ignorance. "I can't tell time, Mommy." She then purchased for his room a digital clock and established *The Law of the Snowman*. "You, sir, don't get out of bed until you see that the first number is a *snowman*."

So once again, we see our need to spurn a passive-purple four-ball mindset. In our personal devotional lives, we can't permit ourselves to be pushed around by our environment. We can't let ourselves be bullied by the world, the flesh, and the Devil. We've got to subdue and rule, so help us God.

1 *The Works of John Owen* (Edinburgh: Banner of Truth [1850-53], reprinted, 1977), p.291
2 Charles Bridges, *Proverbs* (Edinburgh: Banner of Truth, 1979), p.53
3 J.C. Ryle, *Practical Christianity* (Cambridge: James Clark & Co. Ltd., 1970), p.98
4 Ibid., p.62

Chapter 17
Family Devotions

When Isaac aggressively dug and repeatedly unplugged his wells, he did so not only to selfishly hydrate himself, but also to *selflessly* irrigate his whole household. Isaac considered it a solemn obligation to make sure that his family had ample provisions of water to sustain vibrant physical life. What father would be so uncaring as to negligently permit his family to suffer chronic dehydration?

Likewise, the head of a household is solemnly responsible to provide spiritual hydration for his whole household; he is the spiritual "irrigation system" for his family.

> **Ephesians 5:25-27** *Husbands, love your wives, even as Christ also loved the church, and gave himself for it; 26 That he might sanctify and cleanse it with the washing of water by the word, 27 That he might present it to himself a glorious church, not having spot, or wrinkle, or any such thing; but that it should be holy and without blemish.*

That's right! Our wives are our assigned fields whose souls we're to conscientiously cultivate and irrigate with the hoe and water of the Word. And each child composes an additional field that the Lord has solemnly assigned to our estates.

> **Ephesians 6:4** *And, fathers, do not provoke your children to anger; but bring them up in the discipline and instruction of the Lord.*

What father would be so uncaring as to negligently permit his family to suffer chronic dehydration of their souls? A loving and godly man will make it a conscientious priority to spiritually nurture every soul that has been appointed to his care.

I believe that the best, most efficient, and most biblical method for spiritually watering our households, is for us as husbands and fathers to commit ourselves to habitually gathering together our broods for family devotions. Practically speaking, I mean that men should gather their families around the breakfast table, or the dinner table, or in a living room, for the purpose of:

1. Bringing instruction from the Scriptures by way of reading and commenting from an open Bible or from a spiritual book.

2. Bringing praises to God by the singing of a psalm, hymn, or spiritual song.

3. Bringing prayers before the Lord by a heartfelt petitioning for needed family graces and mercies.

An episode of God-honoring family devotions has no inspired duration. It may, due to scheduling crunch, be as brief as ten minutes. At other times, it may be joyfully extended to forty minutes or more.

The Scriptures should chisel our convictions regarding our establishing an habitual family altar or consistent family devotions. I believe the Lord has clearly given a mandate to heads of households in this matter.

> **Genesis 4:26** *And to Seth, to him also a son was born; and he called his name Enosh. Then men began to call upon the name of the LORD.*

Regarding this Genesis record, J. H. Merle d'Aubigne writes:

> It is evident that the first worship which the first man and his children paid to God could be nothing else than *family worship*, since they constituted the only group which then existed on the earth.[1]

Wherever Abraham *pitched his tent*, he *built an altar*, next to his residence, for the purpose of worship.

> **Genesis 12:7-8** *And the LORD appeared to Abram and said, "To your descendants I will give this land." So he built an altar there to the LORD who had appeared to him. 8 Then he proceeded from there to the moun-*

tain on the east of Bethel, and pitched his tent, with Bethel on the west and Ai on the east; and there he built an altar to the LORD and called upon the name of the LORD.

Genesis 13:3-4 *And he went on his journeys from the Negev as far as Bethel, to the place where his tent had been at the beginning, between Bethel and Ai, 4 to the place of the altar, which he had made there formerly; and there Abram called on the name of the LORD.*

Genesis 13:18 *Then Abram moved his tent and came and dwelt by the oaks of Mamre, which are in Hebron, and there he built an altar to the LORD.*

Abraham, the father of the faithful, was solemnly commissioned by God to take aggressive measures to assertively teach and cultivate heart godliness in his offspring.

Genesis 18:19 *"For I have chosen him, in order that he may command his children and his household after him to keep the way of the LORD by doing righteousness and justice; in order that the LORD may bring upon Abraham what He has spoken about him."*

God-fearing parents also are assigned the task of continuously communicating the words of God to their children:

Deuteronomy 6:6-9 *And these words, which I command thee this day, shall be in thine heart: 7 And thou shalt teach them diligently unto thy children, and shalt talk of them when thou sittest in thine house, and when thou walkest by the way, and when thou liest down, and when thou risest up. 8 And thou shalt bind them for a sign upon thine hand, and they shall be as frontlets between thine eyes. 9 And thou shalt write them upon the posts of thy house, and on thy gates.*

The godly man, Job, habitually sent for his brood and gathered them around an altar of worship, with Daddy acting as the prophet and priest:

Job 1:4-5 *And his sons went and feasted in their houses, every one his day; and sent and called for their three sisters to eat and to drink with them. 5 And it was so, when the days of their feasting were gone about, that Job*

> *sent and sanctified them, and rose up early in the morning, and offered burnt offerings according to the number of them all: for Job said, It may be that my sons have sinned, and cursed God in their hearts. Thus did Job continually.*

Parents have a holy obligation to tell with their own mouths to the next generation of the great acts of God and his redemption:

> **Psalm 78:3-4** *Which we have heard and known, And our fathers have told us. 4 We will not conceal them from their children, But tell to the generation to come the praises of the LORD, And His strength and His wondrous works that He has done.*

What's more, fathers should be a river of verbal instruction directing his children in the ways of godliness. He gives to his sons truckloads of spiritual teaching on every conceivable topic:

> **Proverbs 1:8-10** *Hear, my son, your father's instruction, And do not forsake your mother's teaching; 9 Indeed, they are a graceful wreath to your head, And ornaments about your neck. 10 My son, if sinners entice you, do not consent.*

> **Proverbs 3:1** *My son, do not forget my teaching,*

> **Proverbs 4:1** *Hear, O sons, the instruction of a father,*

> **Proverbs 4:10** *Hear, my son, and accept my sayings,*

> **Proverbs 5:1** *My son, give attention to my wisdom, Incline your ear to my understanding;*

> **Proverbs 5:7** *Now then, my sons, listen to me, And do not depart from the words of my mouth.*

When do ***your*** children get this blessed deposit of wisdom and instruction from *your mouth*? Are you to them a fresh-flowing river, or a dried-out stream bed? When do you make the time to teach them the Bible and its spiritual principles? I'm willing to wager that if you haven't carved out a pattern of consistent and habitual family devotions, your family suffers from negligence, and exists in spiritually drought-stricken conditions. Could it be that your, "O, I teach them *whenever*" policy, in actuality amounts to an "I teach them *never*" reality?

Please, let me persuade you to resolve to *schedule into your family life* a consistent habit of family devotions. As J.W. Alexander so thoughtfully writes:

> Summon a family to the worship of God, at stated hours, and you summon each one to a seriousness of reflection, of which he might have been wholly robbed, by the hurry of the day's business.[2]

In the activities of every day, there are many things useful, but only one thing needful (Luke 10:41-42). The one thing needful for our families is the keeping of our hearts in a healthy condition before the Lord. *Soul cultivation* needs to be our chief priority. But sadly, through parental negligence, many families have become spiritually run down like the proverbial sluggard's vineyard.

> **Proverbs 24:30-33** *I passed by the field of the sluggard, And by the vineyard of the man lacking sense; 31 And behold, it was completely overgrown with thistles, Its surface was covered with nettles, And its stone wall was broken down. 32 When I saw, I reflected upon it; I looked, and received instruction. 33 "A little sleep, a little slumber, A little folding of the hands to rest," 34 Then your poverty will come as a robber, And your want like an armed man.*

Let's admit it, it's very easy to become *passive* and lazy when it comes to taking care of the vineyard of souls to which the Lord has assigned us. It's the twenty-first century. Our families rise early and are typically off to the four winds. One goes to work, one to school, while another goes shopping. There are lessons to take, athletic practices and games to play, dinners to make, newspapers to read, homework to be done, ballgames to be watched, telephone calls to make, relaxation to be enjoyed, and bedtimes to be met. With this kind of high intensity lifestyle, it's very easy for a man to chronically fail to take control of his family's spiritual life and summon all together for a time of family devotions. It's quite easy for a series of devotionless days to become a devotionless week, then a devotionless month, then a basically devotionless year, and ultimately a basically devotionless upbringing in your home. What a tragedy! Don't let it happen.

Let's reason together. A child born into your family has approximately twenty years to live under your roof. That translates into 7300 potential days for pouring into his thirsty mind the waters of biblical instruction. Let's liken his soul capacity to an Olympic-size swimming pool. If each day, you poured a large pail of water into the pool, by the end of the twenty years, you'd have some real depth. It would be nearly full to the brim. On the other hand, if you forgot to pour on half the days, the pool would hardly be swimmable. If you neglected pouring on most of the days, the pool would only be wadeable. Do we want our children to have spiritual depth? Or are we content for them to be spiritually shallow?

The decision is ours: Whether we will or will not aggressively exercise godly dominion over the schedules of our families. "Will I this day discipline myself and my family's agenda to address the one thing needful? Will I today pour in the daily pailful?"

We need to adopt the *work ethic* of our Lord Jesus who only had a brief window of time in which to do the work the Father had assigned Him.

> **John 9:4** *We must work the works of Him who sent Me, as long as it is day; night is coming, when no man can work.*

Before you know it, your children will be gone and out of your house. The brief day of your parenting will soon be over. We must do our work while it's still day. For some readers, the day is *already well spent. Today* is the day to start pouring. Let's gird ourselves as men of dominion and grab hold of this solemn chore to "irrigate" our families with the Word.

Premeditatedly make a plan and then resolve to carry it through. For our family, and myself, the dinner table provides the best location and time. We're typically all together already. Mealtime is full of lively eating and discussing. Before anybody leaves the table, we have family devotions. The devotion Bibles are stored right there in a bookshelf, within reach. This avoids the need for each family member leaving the table to hunt for and retrieve his Bible from who knows where.

We read, comment, ask questions, give applications, and press implications. We typically move consecutively through whole biblical books, about a chapter per day. When the children were younger, we used picture books and even acted out many biblical narratives. Occasionally we'll vary our diet and read from a short biography, *Pilgrim's Progress*, or a book on some topical issue. We don't sing as often as my wife would like us to, and as often as we should. Then we always end in a brief time of prayer.

This is the way we do it. You can do it your own way. But the crucial issue is, do it some way! *Have a plan.* There are many published practical materials available to assist you in this great work.

Philip Henry, the father of the great pastor and commentator Matthew Henry, gave himself wholeheartedly to consistent, daily family worship. It's no surprise that his son became a man of great spiritual depth. Matthew writes about his father's earthy and practical views on the subject:

> He made conscience, and made a business of family worship, in all the parts of it; and in it he was uniform, steady, and constant from the time that he was first called to the charge of a family, to his dying day; and, according to his own practice, he took all occasions to press it upon others. His doctrine, from Joshua 25:15, was that family-worship is family-duty. He would say, sometimes, if the worship of God be not in the house, write: "Lord, have mercy on us, on the door; for there is a plague, a curse in that house. . ."
>
> He that makes his house a little church, shall find that God will make it a little sanctuary. . . He was ever careful to have all his family present at family-worship; . . . yet he would sometimes say, "Better one away, than all sleepy." . . . In the tabernacle the priests were every day to *burn incense*, and to *light the lamps*; the former figuring the duty of prayer, the latter the duty of reading the word. . . .
>
> He recommended that the wife should sometimes be called upon [to conduct family worship], especially in the husband's absence. . . . *It is comfortable if the moon rises when the sun sets. . . .*
>
> When sometimes he had hit upon some useful observation that was new to him, he would say afterwards to those about him, "How often have I read this chapter, and never before now took notice of such a thing in it!" . . .
>
> He managed his daily family worship, so as to make it a pleasure, and not a task to his children and servants; for he was seldom long, and never tedious in the service; the variety made it pleasant; so that none who joined with him had ever any reason to say, "Behold, what a

> weariness is it!" Such an excellent ability he had of rendering religion the most sweet and amiable employment in the world; and so careful was he, like Jacob, *to drive as the children could go*, not putting *new wine into old bottles.*[3]

Let me underscore Henry's priority of making the devotional time sweet and pleasant. Some families have practiced family worship as a rigid, stiff, bland form. I strongly discourage such an approach.

> **Proverbs 15:2a** *The tongue of the wise makes knowledge acceptable...*

> **Proverbs 16:21-24** *The wise in heart will be called discerning, and sweetness of speech increases persuasiveness. 23 The heart of the wise teaches his mouth, And adds persuasiveness to his lips. 24 Pleasant words are a honeycomb, Sweet to the soul and healing to the bones.*

Some of our family's most enjoyable, laughing-to-tears-times, have been during times of family devotions. We'll never forget the evening that the theme of *Justification by Faith* took us on a field trip out into the backyard, where the perfectly white T-shirt was dipped into the wading pool, then ground into the filthy black dirt, illustrating first the righteousness of Christ and then the unrighteousness of sinners. Yes, our righteous deeds are as *filthy rags*. But Christ's righteousness is spotless and unblemished. Be creative. Make sure you're connecting with the children.

You'll find that your family devotions will become an invaluable forum for dealing with vital issues such as honesty, night-time fears, depression, insecurity, peer pressure, companions, heaven and hell, money management, tithing, sibling strife, bullies, retaliation, sharing, heroism, sovereignty and free will, crude speech, dating, sexual purity, modest dress, hard work, laziness, self control, sympathy for the underdog, pride, bad calls by referees and umpires, feminism, capital punishment, death and assurance of salvation. The list goes on and on.

Imagine, after twenty years of this kind of a curriculum, the depth of biblical insight your offspring can enjoy. Don't waste this invaluable window of opportunity by negligently lounging back like a pathetic *passive-purple four-ball!*

Let me "connect the dots" regarding our personal devotions and our family devotions. If the head of the household conscientiously maintains the well of his own soul, he will have the heart source from which he will be able to draw refreshing waters for his family. But if a husband/father's heart is passively neglected and permitted to dry up, his "irrigation" duties toward his family will result in their spiritual dehydration.

Consider again the words of J. W. Alexander:

> There is no member of a household whose individual piety is of such importance to all the rest, as the father or head; and there is no one whose soul is so directly influenced by the exercise of family worship. Where the head of a family is lukewarm or worldly, he will send the chill through the whole house; and if any happy exception occur, and one and another surpass him in faithfulness, it will be in spite of his evil example. . . . Where the head of the family is a man of faith, of affection, and of zeal, consecrating all his works and life to Christ, it is very rare to find all his household otherwise minded.[4]

May the Lord help us to exercise a manly dominion over our family devotions.

1 J.H. Merle d'Aubigne, *Family Worship: Motives and Directions for Domestic Piety*, a sermon preached in Brussels; first published in Paris (reprint: Dallas: Presbyterian Publications, 1989)
2 J.W. Alexander, *Thoughts on Family Worship* ([originally published : 1847] Harrisonburg, VA: Sprinkle Publications, 1991), p.32
3 *The Lives of Philip and Matthew Henry* (Edinburgh: Banner of Truth, 1974), pp.72-79
4 *Thoughts on Family Worship*, p.33

Chapter 18
Churchmanship

Another important sphere that cries out for the implementation of manly dominion principles, is the area of Churchmanship. Passive-purple-four-ballism is shamefully evident in the attitude most modern professing Christians have toward the local church. Prevailing attitudes toward church attendance, worship, ministry, and commitment are of the, "I'll participate if *I feel like it*" variety.

Imagine with me: One Monday night, Mickey receives a phone call. It's Joe, asking Mickey if he'll play shortstop on the softball team for the city league. Mickey pauses for a moment, thinking through his swarming responsibilities and busy schedule. He responds this way: "I'll tell you what, Joe, put me on the team, as long as I don't have to pay anything, come to any practices, or commit to being at every game. Sorry about my being so cheap and uncommitted about it, but if it costs me anything, I'd just as soon not play."

Joe, desperate to fill out his roster, answers, "Hey, we'll take what we can get. I'll put you down."

Mickey's cheap and uncommitted allegiance toward the softball team well reflects many people's cheap and uncommitted allegiance toward the local church. "I'll participate as long as *I feel like it*, and as long as *it's cheap*. As long as it's *convenient* and *pleasant*, I'll partake. But if you're asking me to miss some of my entertainment, rearrange my weekends, weary my body, reprioritize my life, or deny myself, then I'm not really interested."

Multitudes view their duty toward the church as fluctuating with their feelings: "As a passive tumbleweed in the wind of my feelings, I come to church when I feel like it. I'll worship there if, and as long as, it makes me feel good. I'll participate in the ministry as long as I feel it's meeting my needs."

In response, most modern churches cater to "feeling-driven purple four-balls." Churches have adopted a pragmatism based on *user friendliness.* No longer is the church a *sacred house* where worshipers come to serve the Lord. Now the church has become an *amusement park* where thrill-seekers come to amuse themselves. That's why many churches resemble a *theatre* ("We'll entertain you."), a *talent show* ("We'll give you a place on the stage."), a *lounge* ("We'll make you feel relaxed."), a *spa* ("Come only when you feel like it."), or a *country club* ("We'll provide activities for the whole family.").

This pop culture perversion of the church has conditioned many to assume a spoiled consumer's attitude: "What do you offer for me today?" In striking contrast, the Scriptures call us to take on a *valiant servant's attitude*: "How can I serve the Lord today?"

When David was about to offer up the first sacrifice at the eventual temple site in Jerusalem, Araunah the Jebusite offered his land, oxen, and firewood to David *free of charge.* But David, who had a valiant servant's attitude toward God-honoring sacrifice, responded with an insistence on expensively *spending himself* in his worship.

> **2 Samuel 24:18-25** *So Gad came to David that day and said to him, "Go up, erect an altar to the LORD on the threshing floor of Araunah the Jebusite." 19 And David went up according to the word of Gad, just as the LORD had commanded. 20 And Araunah looked down and saw the king and his servants crossing over toward him; and Araunah went out and bowed his face to the ground before the king. 21 Then Araunah said, "Why has my lord the king come to his servant?" And David said," To buy the threshing floor from you, in order to build an altar to the LORD, that the plague may be held back from the people. " 22 And Araunah said to David, "Let my lord the king take and offer up what is good in his sight. Look, the oxen for the burnt offering, the threshing sledges and the yokes of the oxen for the wood. 23 "Everything, O king, Araunah gives to the king." And Araunah said to the king, "May the LORD your God accept you." 24 However, the king said to Araunah, "No, but I will surely buy it from you for a price, for I will not offer burnt offerings to the LORD my God which cost me nothing." So David bought the threshing floor and the oxen for fifty shekels of silver. 25 And David built there an altar to the LORD, and offered burnt offerings and peace offerings. Thus the LORD was moved by entreaty for the land, and the plague was held back from Israel.*

Here, David states a fundamental principle that should mark all God-honoring worship in both the Lord's old covenant house (the temple) and new covenant house (the church).

> **2 Sam 24:34b** *"I will not offer burnt offerings to the LORD my God which cost me nothing."*

David's worship slogan must be ours! Church worship and service must not be engaged in *passively* and *cheaply*. We must resolve to be aggressive and expensive in our public devotion to our Lord.

Passive, "come when I feel like it," low priority, *cheap* churchmanship is an offense to our Savior whom we claim to worship. How much did it cost Jesus to coerce justice to sheathe its sword against us as sinners? It cost Jesus the heavy price of his own lifeblood poured out on the cross. The sincere Christian thinks: "The sword of justice that I deserved to have run through me for eternity in Hell, ran through my Lord Jesus on Golgotha."

> *Death's dark angel sheathes his sword.*
> — (Robert Campbell, *At the Lamb's High Feast We Sing*, verse 2)

The love of Christ constrains the Christian to dispose of half-hearted, passive churchmanship, and adopt David's wholehearted slogan.

> "I will not offer burnt offerings to the LORD my God which cost me nothing."

The following are comments on David's worship/churchmanship slogan of 2 Samuel 24:

> R. C. Trench: "That which costs nothing is worth nothing."

> Bishop Hall: "It is a heartless piety of those base-minded Christians care only to serve God good and cheap."

> Matthew Henry: "Note, those know not what religion is, whose chief care is to make it cheap and easy on themselves, and who are best pleased with that which costs them least pains."

> Gordon Keddie: "The Lord is not to be offered the dregs of our lives. . . . David's words encapsulate a principle that applies to all worship, offerings, and service to the Lord. The Lord is worthy of our first fruits—the cream—of our lives."[1]

So, it's only fitting that we that we adopt an aggressive, manly dominion mindset to our *churchmanship*. We need to act like motivated men who *subdue* and *rule*.

The following are guidelines for the true churchman:

1. Regarding Attendance

So help me God, my family and I *will be there*. It will be a priority in our schedules. The Lord's Day is *His day* for worship, not *our day* for fun. If my church is holding a Sunday school hour, an AM Worship, and a PM Worship, me and my house will be present. Though I may *feel* like I'd rather stay home and read my Wednesday night paper, I'll make it to prayer meeting.

> **Hebrews 10:25** *not forsaking our own assembling together, as is the habit of some, but encouraging one another; and all the more, as you see the day drawing near.*

Why is it that we'd be *religiously careful* to make sure that our child doesn't miss any soccer practices or games, but *sloppily careless* in permitting ourselves to miss frequent church services? We'd never miss work or class because of a sniffle. Why is a sniffle an excuse for missing worship? Why should our employer get higher priority treatment than our Savior?

2. Regarding Worship

So help me God, I will not passively sit back in my pew, waiting to be entertained, but will gird up the loins of my mind, and expend *concentration energy* as I worship in Spirit and in truth. The old covenant priests who served in the temple drenched themselves in sweat as they prepared and offered up their appointed sacrifices. We, as new covenant priests in the church, must be willing to pour out mental sweat. We must be willing to put out energy as we conscientiously concentrate on the public prayers, the Scripture readings, and the hymn lyrics.

We shouldn't expect the preacher or teacher to entertain us, but should be willing to isometrically press our minds against his for the full duration of the sermon. If we can give our full attention for over three consecutive hours to watching a baseball or football game, surely we can give nearly an hour to listening to God's word preached.

Remember, dumbed-down sermonettes produce dumbed-down Christianettes. The pagan world gets well over one-hundred hours of our waking attention per week. Why should we begrudge the preached Word getting two hours of our full attention in the same span?

3. Regarding Service

So help me God, I will sacrificially give myself to serving my local church ministry. I've been privileged to watch some of Christ's choicest servants selflessly give themselves year after year to serving in many out-of-the-limelight, low-profile places in the church. When we long ago rented the facilities of a Christian school in Holland, one of our men would stay behind every Sunday night, getting down on his hands and knees, to scrub every scuff mark from the hallway tile floors in order to leave a good testimony with the school.

A valiant churchman willingly serves his turn in the nursery, and sometimes cheerfully fills in when somebody else forgets. He volunteers to drive the older handicapped saint to church. He's willing to burn the Saturday midnight oil to teach a children's Sunday school class. He's willing to habitually go beyond the comfort zone of his familiar friends in order to greet and meet visitors, and even invite them over to his home for hospitality. He receives from His Savior and Lord the, "Well done, thou good and faithful servant."

4. Regarding Public Praying

So help me God, I will not give in to my personal insecurities and inhibitions, but will take up my solemn duty to carry my share of the load by leading the congregation in prayer.

About a year ago, a young man in our church confided in me that he had a strong aversion to leading in public prayer. He asked, therefore, that I not call on him to do so. I told him that I didn't believe I would be his friend if I granted this request. I encouraged him to *subdue* and *rule* over his shyness and inhibitions. I told him that the Lord Jesus didn't want eloquence, but only sincerity. Within a month, this dear young man, of his own accord, stepped up and led during an *open session* of public prayer. His words weren't profound, but they were precious. His manly voice is now commonly heard among us at the Throne of Grace.

5. Regarding Financial Giving

So help me God, I will give faithfully and sacrificially to the cause of Your church and Your kingdom.

Near my home is a church that often places profound sayings on its front yard sign. One week it read: "Forget honking, how about tithing!" Of course, it was alluding to the popular slogan, "Honk, if you love Jesus!"

I'm not here begging for dollars, as many media ministries tend to do. I'm merely summoning us to fulfill our solemn financial obligation toward the *local churches* of Christ. Yes, I believe the Old Testament tithe (ten percent of one's income) is presented as the biblical norm for basic giving. It, the tithe, belongs to the Lord.

> **Leviticus 27:30** *'Thus all the tithe of the land, of the seed of the land or of the fruit of the tree, is the LORD'S; it is holy to the LORD.*

Don't forget that this Old Testament "tithe" which supported the Levites, is the very same "*share*" that the New Testament Paul is referring to when he speaks of the Corinthians' obligation to support the *local church* and its ministry.

> **1 Corinthians 9:13-14** *Do you not know that those who perform sacred services eat the food of the temple, and those who attend regularly to the altar have their share with the altar? 14 So also the Lord directed those who proclaim the gospel to get their living from the gospel.*

This "tithe" percentage should be the beginning of our giving, to which should be added additional offerings according to our ability and the willingness of our hearts (2 Corinthians 8:1-5). Faithfulness in this biblical practice would strengthen many financially limping *local churches* and enable them to move mountains of evil.

> To pluck a weed from the roadside and present it to a sovereign would be no better than an insult. Yet how often is God served with that which costs men nothing! Men that will lavish hundreds and thousands to gratify their own fancy, what miserable driblets they often give to the

> cause of God! The smallest of coins is good enough for His treasury.[2]

> "I will not offer burnt offerings to the LORD my God which cost me nothing."

Let me close this chapter by making a plea for Christians to find and join churches that embrace and cultivate a *manly dominion* view of *Churchmanship*. If you can't help reform your own local church, find and join one, or establish one, that views the church not as a *spa*, but as a *gymnasium*. Let me expand on this.

I've frequently visit the local high school where two of my sons have attended and played sports. Most frequently, I've visited the gymnasium. There, I've seen football and soccer players pumping iron, basketball players practicing lay-ups, wrestlers pounding one another into the mats, volleyball players practicing sets and spikes, cross country runners circling the field house, baseball players fielding ground balls, high jumpers pushing for that extra inch; and swimmers doing laps to overcome burning lungs.

In the gymnasium, they're always *pushing one another* to higher levels of achievement. Unlike a spa, a gymnasium is not a place for leisurely relaxation. It's a body-disciplining facility. Regarding the church assembling together, the writer to the Hebrews says:

> **Hebrews 10:24-25** *and let us consider how to <u>stimulate one another</u> to love and good deeds, 25 not forsaking our own <u>assembling together</u>, as is the habit of some, but <u>encouraging one another</u>; and all the more, as you see the day drawing near.*

This *stimulating one another*, or spurring one another on to higher achievement reminds me of a gymnasium weight room scene I witnessed. The red-faced bench presser was straining and wanted to quit. But his spotter (helper) refused to assist him in lifting the bar and shouted, "Come on! One more! You can do it!" And he did! I've seen the same thing in the pool as a swimmer's teammates cheer him down the home stretch to higher levels of performance.

We need to be in churches that stimulate and spur us on to higher levels of godliness. The word *gymnasium* comes from the Greek words *gumnazo*. It fundamentally means, "be naked." In Greek gymnasiums the athletes would throw off all clothing encumbrances in their vigorous training. Paul uses the same root when he writes to Timothy:

> **1 Timothy 4:7b-8** *discipline (gumnazo) yourself for the purpose of godliness; 8 for bodily discipline (gumnasia) is only of little profit, but godliness is profitable for all things, since it holds promise for the present life and also for the life to come.*

Regarding the need to listen more carefully to some pretty intense theological teaching about Melchizedek, the writer to the Hebrews says:

> **Hebrews 5:11-14** *Concerning him (Melchizedek) we have much to say, and it is hard to explain, since you have become dull of hearing. 12 For though by this time you ought to be teachers, you have need again for someone to teach you the elementary principles of the oracles of God, and you have come to need milk and not solid food. 13 For everyone who partakes only of milk is not accustomed to the word of righteousness, for he is a babe. 14 But solid food is for the mature, who because of practice have their senses trained (gumnazo) to discern good and evil.*

The New Testament calls us to take an *athletic* approach toward driving one another on toward spiritual excellence:

> **1 Corinthians 9:24-27** *Do you not know that those who run in a race all run, but only one receives the prize? Run in such a way that you may win. 25 And everyone who competes in the games exercises self-control in all things. They then do it to receive a perishable wreath, but we an imperishable. 26 Therefore I run in such a way, as not without aim; I box in such a way, as not beating the air; 27 but I buffet my body and make it my slave, lest possibly, after I have preached to others, I myself should be disqualified.*

Christians should avoid contemporary, pragmatic churches that model themselves after an entertainment *theatre*, a talent *show*, a relaxation *lounge*, a feel-good *spa*, or a *country club*. Instead, Christians should become a part of churches that biblically model themselves after a *gymnasium*.

May it never be said that Olympians drive themselves harder to get their rusting medals than the Christians of our churches push themselves to get their *imperishable crowns*. May we resolve not to be satisfied with being part of a church that is a pampering spa of spiritually flabby, sluggardly professing Christians, who make us feel good, because we fit right in with them. Instead, let's resolve to seek out a spiritually challenging gym, where Christians have "the eye of the tiger," and say:

> **Philippians 3:12-14** *Not as though I had already attained, either were already perfect: but I follow after, if that I may apprehend that for which also I am apprehended of Christ Jesus. 13 Brethren, I count not myself to have apprehended: but this one thing I do, forgetting those things which are behind, and reaching forth unto those things which are before, 14 I press toward the mark for the prize of the high calling of God in Christ Jesus.*

We should long to be in a church where Christian brothers and sisters come alongside one another and say, "Come on, friend, you can do one more! Don't quit now! You can get the upper hand on one more sin! You can establish one more godly habit in your life! The Spirit of God will help you do this!"

May the Lord help us to *subdue* and *rule* in our churchmanship.

1 Gorden Keddie, *Triumph of the King, Welwyn Commentary Series* (Darlington, UK: Evangelical Press, 1990), p.245

2 W.G. Blaikie, *The Second Book of Samuel* (Minneapolis: Klock&Klock Publishers, [originally published, 1893], reprint, 1983), p.387

Chapter 19
Conversion

I don't want to assume anything. Surely some eyes that have reached this page belong to souls who are not yet Christians. You may claim to be an atheist or an agnostic. Maybe you're a Muslim or a Hindu. Maybe you attend a church every Sunday and faithfully participate in religious ceremonies. Possibly you're even a member in good standing of a faithful Bible-believing and teaching church. But the bottom line in your case is that *you're not a genuine Christian*, and you know it, or at least you strongly suspect it.

Then you've got work to do—heart work! It's not time for passive-purple-four-ball procrastination. It's time for manly dominion. In life, every man has one chief errand to get done—to get right with God! Since life is so short, what we do, we need to do quickly.

The Lord Jesus gave us that prudent work ethic:

> **John 9:4** "*We must work the works of Him who sent Me, as long as it is day;* <u>*night is coming*</u>*, when no man can work.*

The point is that night will creep up on each of us far more swiftly than we'd imagined. And if our *chief errand* has been neglected, it would be better for us if we'd never been born.

Consider this parable. A fifteen-year-old was an outstanding soccer player. We'll call him James. His team was scheduled to play in a prestigious national tournament in Cincinnati in late July. All year, James was looking forward to this weekend as the chance for his team to romp, and he himself to be seen by the scouts. He couldn't wait.

Early Wednesday morning, James' Dad poked his head into his son's bedroom and said, "Hey James, I told you on Monday that you're not going to Cincinnati unless that lawn is done perfectly, no streaks." James' family had a three-acre lawn, and his Dad required golf course quality mowing with no missed "stripes." As James lay there in bed, he knew that the team was leaving before dawn on Thursday, and understood Dad was telling him to get it done today. "Yup, I know," groaned James, "I'll get it done." But when Dad came down an hour later, James was still sleeping. "James! You better get moving, pal!" Another hour later, Dad finds James playing a computer game. "James, it's midmorning!" Without looking away from the screen, James says, "Don't worry, Dad, I've got plenty of time!" Just before lunch, Dad finds James watching TV, and just shakes his head. After lunch, James gets a call from the guys who want him to play some two-on-two basketball. As he's heading down the driveway in his friend's car, his Dad asks, "When are you going to hit that lawn?" Irritated, James snaps, "Dad, I've got plenty of time, don't worry about it!" And away he went.

The two-on-two was great. They watched some ESPN. Linda called and asked if they wanted to come over and swim in her pool. Afterwards everybody went out for some burgers and had a great time. Well after 8:00 pm as James was being driven up his driveway, he saw his Dad standing with his hands on his hips. James had forgotten completely! The sun was getting pretty low.

In a panic, James ran into the garage and fired up the aging—and headlightless—John Deere. After about an acre, James' father heard his son mumbling hysterically in the dark: "I can't see the rows!" Reluctantly, Dad walked out into the yard and shut off the mower. Staring at James, he said, "You squandered the day, now you miss the tournament."

The stakes related to your salvation and conversion are a lot higher than missing a tournament. It's missing heaven and going to hell. I will spare you the description of the panic you'll feel when you're somewhere at the dusk of your life in a position where you've still got a lot of heart work to do.

I was once at the hospital bedside of a dying man whose family asked me to come and urge him to repent and trust in Christ. He was thrashing in bed with conscience convulsions. He was dreading dying. His sins had come to haunt him. But death's fever and the morphine had so clouded his mind that it was too dark to work. He couldn't see the lines anymore. Within a few hours, he slipped into eternity.

Oh, but you're healthy and young! You've got plenty of time, right? Many a young life has been shortened by a sudden accident or illness. Act now—while you can still see the lines! Do it now. Put the book down right after this chapter, and get right with God.

> "Swift to its close ebbs out life's little day . . . ."
> —Henry Lyte, *Abide With Me*

Bow your head now before Almighty God and plead with Him in the Name of the Lord Jesus Christ to have mercy on your hell-deserving soul.

You were conceived a sinner in your mother's womb. Adam's guilt was charged to your account. You were born condemned in sin. As you grew and matured, you seconded Adam's rebellion with your own hand, mouth, and mind. You've sinned continuously against God's law in thought, word, and action. You've worshipped yourself and the world. You've chiseled out God according to your own liking. You've cursed with God's name. You've trampled God's day. You've defied, deceived, and dishonored your parents. You've murdered people by hating them in your heart. Your lusts make you guilty of perverse sexual sin. You've stolen incalculable dollars of time, money and goods, haven't you? You're a liar. You've been obsessed with wanting forbidden fruit.

With those heavy millstones of sins tied around your neck, you're doomed to split hell wide open. You've got a *bad record*, and a *bad heart*, which just keeps producing more sin. If you try to *clean up your act* by doing good deeds to make up for the bad deeds, it's a fool's errand:

> **Isaiah 64:6** *For all of us have become like one who is unclean, And all our righteous deeds are like a filthy garment; And all of us wither like a leaf, And our iniquities, like the wind, take us away.*

If we're to be acquitted on Judgment Day, we must be spotlessly righteous in the sight of God. A single moral blemish will disqualify us from heaven and send us to hell:

> **Romans 3:19-23** *Now we know that whatever the Law says, it speaks to*

those who are under the Law, that every mouth may be closed, and all the world may become accountable to God; 20 because by the works of the Law no flesh will be justified in His sight; for through the Law comes the knowledge of sin. . . . 23 for all have sinned and fall short of the glory of God.

Some years ago two men were in a boat and found themselves unable to manage the stupendous falls of Niagara. Persons on the shore saw them but were unable to do much for their rescue. At last, however, one man was saved by floating a rope to him which he grasped. The same instant the rope came into his hand, a log floated by the other man. Instead of seizing the rope, he laid hold on the log. It was a fatal mistake. The one was drawn to shore because he had a connection with the people on the land, while the other, clinging to the log, was borne irresistibly along, and was never heard of afterwards.

Do you see here a practical illustration? Faith is connection with Christ. Christ is on the shore, so to speak, holding the rope of faith, and if we lay hold of it with the hand of our confidence, he pulls us to shore. But our good works, having no connection with Christ, are dirtied along down the gulf of despair. Grapple them as tightly as we may, even with hooks of steel, they cannot avail us in the least degree.[1]

We can't save ourselves by our good works. But Jesus Christ came to do what we couldn't do. He is the perfect and unblemished Lamb of God who takes away the sins of the world. He was born without sin and lived without sin. On the cross he became a beast of burden scapegoat. There on his back, he bore the load of sinners.

Come, right now, and know your sins. Own your sins. Be ashamed of your sins. Confess your sins. Lay your sins by faith on Jesus.

I lay my sins on Jesus, the spotless Lamb of God;
He bears them all, and frees us, from the accursed load;
I bring my guilt to Jesus, to wash my crimson stains
White in his blood most precious, till not a spot remains.
— Horatius Bonar, Trinity Hymnal, *#430* verse 1

Romans 3:21-28 *But now apart from the Law the righteousness of God has been manifested, being witnessed by the Law and the Prophets, 22 even the righteousness of God through faith in Jesus Christ for all those who believe; for there is no distinction; 23 for all have sinned and fall*

> *short of the glory of God, 24 being justified as a gift by His grace through the redemption which is in Christ Jesus; 25 whom God displayed publicly as a propitiation in His blood through faith. This was to demonstrate His righteousness, because in the forbearance of God He passed over the sins previously committed; 26 for the demonstration, I say, of His righteousness at the present time, that He might be just and the justifier of the one who has faith in Jesus. 27 Where then is boasting? It is excluded. By what kind of law? Of works? No, but by a law of faith. 28 For we maintain that a man is justified by faith apart from works of the Law.*

The Lord Jesus wore sinners' filthy rags on *Crucifixion Day*, that by faith, they might wear His fine linen on *Judgment Day*. This is the wonderfully manifested righteousness of God—Christ's righteousness.

Come, today, abandon all your "do-goodery" efforts to save yourself. It's a fool's errand. By faith, lay all of your sins on Jesus, and believe in Him as your Lamb, who was slain in the place of sinners, who drank the cup of wrath sinners deserve down to the last drop, saying, "It is finished." Believe in the Lord Jesus, and not a drop remains for you to drink on Judgment Day. For you, hell will be extinguished; heaven will be yours.

"But," you may ask, "How can I know if I'm really saved?" You may know of people who claim to believe in Christ, but practically live in habitual disobedience to Him. There's *no fruit*. There's *no evidence* of the Holy Spirit's indwelling the professing believer, making him a holy man.

An old preacher told of a long row of small houses cheaply built for factory workers. He said that on a winter's day, one could quickly determine by looking at the roofs, which homes were vacant and which were inhabited. The vacant homes were snow covered, having no fire within. The inhabited homes were bare shingled, the warmth of the hearth melting the white blanket. If you're genuinely saved, the Holy Spirit lives in you as a down payment of your salvation. His presence will be observable as He'll warm your soul to the things of God, resulting in the gradual melting away of patterns of sin. He produces a love for the Savior and a hatred for sin.

> **Galatians 5:19-25** *Now the deeds of the flesh are evident, which are: immorality, impurity, sensuality, 20 idolatry, sorcery, enmities, strife, jealousy, outbursts of anger, disputes, dissensions, factions, 21 envying,*

drunkenness, carousing, and things like these, of which I forewarn you just as I have forewarned you that those who practice such things shall not inherit the kingdom of God. 22 But the fruit of the Spirit is love, joy, peace, patience, kindness, goodness, faithfulness, 23 gentleness, self-control; against such things there is no law. 24 Now those who belong to Christ Jesus have crucified the flesh with its passions and desires. 25 If we live by the Spirit, let us also walk by the Spirit.

Luke 6:44 *For each tree is known by its own fruit.*

If your life is blanketed with habits and patterns of sin, if your heart is consistently hard and cold to the Bible's urgings and warnings, if your soul is a stranger to the Spirit's stirring up within you a love of Christ that desires to obey His Word, then you have good reason to wonder if you are really a Christian. You have good reason to doubt your salvation.

2 Corinthians 13:5 *Test yourselves to see if you are in the faith; examine yourselves! Or do you not recognize this about yourselves, that Jesus Christ is in you— unless indeed you fail the test?*

Many years ago, I knew a man named John. He claimed to be a born-again Christian. He talked much about his love for the Lord. But John habitually smoked marijuana, took God's name in vain, and visited the local porn shop. I told him that I feared he was deceiving himself; that he was a "counterfeit Christian," bound not for heaven, but for hell.

Matthew 7:21-23 *"Not everyone who says to Me, 'Lord, Lord,' will enter the kingdom of heaven; but he who does the will of My Father who is in heaven. 22 "Many will say to Me on that day, 'Lord, Lord, did we not prophesy in Your name, and in Your name cast out demons, and in Your name perform many miracles?' 23 "And then I will declare to them, 'I never knew you; DEPART FROM ME, YOU WHO PRACTICE LAWLESSNESS…'"*

Ephesians 5:5 *For this you know with certainty, that no immoral or impure person or covetous man, who is an idolater, has an inheritance in the kingdom of Christ and God. 6 Let no one deceive you with empty*

> *words, for because of these things the wrath of God comes upon the sons of disobedience.*

Habitual toleration of sin patterns rightly diminishes one's assurance of salvation.

Maybe it's obvious that you've got work to do: the *heart work* of repentance. Maybe you've got an offending habit of sin that needs gouging out and cutting off:

> **Mark 9:43** *"And if your hand causes you to stumble, cut it off; it is better for you to enter life crippled, than having your two hands, to go into hell, into the unquenchable fire..."*

Don't passively procrastinate. Aggressively attack the sin. So help you God, put it to death. Go after it today. Repent and believe. His blood can make the foulest clean. Get right with God. The great American preacher Jonathan Edwards put it best:

> "Refuse to rest complacently today in a spiritual condition out of which you know you need to be delivered before you die."

Refuse to say to yourself, "Don't worry, I have plenty of time." You don't. Remember, "Swift to its close ebbs out life's little day." Night is coming, when no man can work.

Put the book down—right now—and go to God.

Manly Dominion in Husbanding

When the Lord created man in the beginning, He assigned Adam to focus his attention on two great concerns:

1. Tending to the Garden

> **Genesis 2:15** *Then the LORD God took the man and put him into the garden of Eden to cultivate it and keep it.*

2. Cleaving to his Wife

> **Genesis 2:22-24** *And the LORD God fashioned into a woman the rib which He had taken from the man, and brought her to the man. 23 And*

> *the man said, "This is now bone of my bones, And flesh of my flesh; She shall be called Woman, Because she was taken out of Man." 24 For this cause a man shall leave his father and his mother, and shall cleave to his wife; and they shall become one flesh.*

Any treatment, therefore, of the theme of manly dominion must of necessity address a man's great assignment of responsibly relating to the precious woman whom the Lord has tailor made as his *helpmate* (Genesis 2:18). Think of it, married man. The Lord has tenderly hand crafted His very own daughter and then entrusted her into your care.

I have four sons and one daughter. My daughter Abigail, this sweet, darling girl, is a most cherished possession of mine. The depths of my love and affections for her are intense and even fierce. I hold the highest of expectations for the young man to whom I would ever give her hand in marriage. Just the thought of it makes my pulse quicken. I'll count on him to husband her with all of his might according to truth and love.

Now, I'm just a sinful man. My daughter-ward love is imperfect. Then, how much more intense are the expectations of the Heavenly Father of us men who've been entrusted with His precious daughters! Surely, we've got to make the husbanding of our wives a chief *priority* of our lives, not an apathetic *afterthought*; and surely the way we husband them, must be according to their Father's Word.

19 / CONVERSION

1 Charles Spurgeon, *Metropolitan Tabernacle, Vol.3* (Pasadena, TX: Pilgrim Publications, 1980), pp. 5-6

Chapter 20
Manly Dominion in Husbanding: Biblical Thinking

Husbands of today have been saturated with the propaganda of *feminism*. As fluoride is everywhere in the water today, *feminism* is everywhere in the air today.

Welden M. Hardenbrook writes in his book, *Missing from Action: Vanishing Manhood in America*:

> Over the years, I have had the privilege of working with the broad spectrum of men who can only be found in America. No matter who they have been—capitalists, Communists, college students, dropouts, Christians, atheists, blacks, whites, young, or old—they have had one problem in common: They have suffered, to one degree or another, from the touch of the *feminizing forces* that have taken over the land. These men have not been sure what it means to be a man. . . . They are men who refuse to take responsibility. Their *passivity* and *inaction* affirm that spiritual *leadership* in their homes belongs to their wives.[1]

The constant imbibing of *feminism*, mixing together with man's native sinfulness, has resulted in an epidemic of passive-purple-four-ballism in modern marriages. Men have permitted themselves to be emasculated into a company of wimp eunuchs, who believe it should be their goal to strive toward being *passive nice guys* in their homes. We've been told, and actually now believe, that "authority" is a naughty word, that male headship is abusive, and that aggressive leadership is rude. Thus, husbands have abdicated the driver's seat and taken a back seat in their marriages.

Adam has become the poster-boy for today's fashionably easy-going husband. Instead of assertively standing at the forefront of his marriage, talking nose to nose with the crafty serpent, he's content to sit back and let Eve do the talking. And when Eve gave her husband the fruit, instead of standing up like a man and boldly refusing to transgress God's Word, he passively caved into the unprincipled and misguided desires of his wife (cf. Genesis 3:1-6). As a result, Adam cursed his family.

This sad Genesis portrait epitomizes most modern marriages. And it's our fault, men! We've got to reject modern thinking and take up biblical thinking. Without apology, the Scriptures teach that the man is to be the leader in his marriage and in his home. *Husbanding* is a crucial endeavor requiring manly dominion.

1. Headship

Yes, the Bible clearly instructs that in marriage, the man is the head over the woman. This means that he is to exercise a real authority over his wife.

> **1 Corinthians 11:3** *But I want you to understand that Christ is the head of every man, <u>and the man is the head of a woman</u>, and God is the head of Christ.*

George Knight, in *The Role Relationship Between Men & Women*, explains:

> The apostles do not argue just for *some authority* in marriage, but explicitly and particularly for *man's authority* and headship over woman and woman's submission to man (Eph. 5:22-33; Col. 3:18-19; 1 Pet. 3:1-7). For the basis of man's headship and woman's submission, the apostle Paul appeals to the analogy of God the Father's headship over Jesus Christ, His incarnate Son (1 Cor. 11:3); to God's creative activity (creating woman from man) and its significance (1 Cor. 11:8-9; see Gen. 2:18-24); and to the analogy of Christ's headship over the church and its submission to Him (Eph. 5:22-33). With full authority and with absolute and permanent reasons, Paul argues for the form of relationship between man and woman.[2]

Man's God-ordained authority was purposefully conveyed as the man was given the prerogative to *name* his wife, "woman" (Genesis 2:23) and "Eve" (Genesis 3:20). Also, the woman's *auxiliary* (assistant) role was clearly displayed in her title as a "helper suitable" or "helpmate" (Genesis 2:18).

So the husband is the God-appointed leader, person in charge, chief in the marriage relationship. The buck stops with the husband. He is to make final decisions, oversee, and delegate as the domestic leader.

But although the husband holds a higher rank of authority than his wife, he shares the same equality of essence with his wife. They are both essentially equal as image bearers of God.

> **Genesis 1:27** *And God created man in His own image, in the image of God He created him; male and female He created them.*

> **Galatians 3:28** *There is neither Jew nor Greek, there is neither slave nor free man, there is neither male nor female; for you are all one in Christ Jesus.*

> **1 Peter 3:7** *You husbands likewise, live with your wives in an understanding way, as with a weaker vessel, since she is a woman; and grant her honor as a fellow heir of the grace of life, so that your prayers may not be hindered.*

Though the husband and wife have *diversity* in rank, they share an *equality* of essence.

Understand, however, that it wasn't with an impulsive whim that God appointed man head over the woman. It wasn't a matter of *eenie, meenie, minie, moe,* if either of the two would perform just as well. On a chessboard, the king and queen could have their functions and positions interchanged without altering the game in the least. This is not true in marriage. By design, God *wired* the mental, emotional, and physical circuitry of men and women to match with their peculiar assignments as head and helpmate.

In 1 Timothy 2:14, Paul argues for man's authority by referring to the Genesis 3 serpent incident:

> And it was not Adam who was deceived, but the woman being quite deceived, fell into transgression.

Could it be that the male's generally more slow, plodding, and logically bent mind (Wife to husband: "Why do you have to be so objective about everything?"), is better suited than the generally more emotional feminine mind, to be a final decision maker? Could it be that male testosterone which produces a bold aggressiveness equips the man for effective leadership? Surely, we're fearfully and wonderfully tailor made for our complementing roles.

Now, this is not to say that a man is not to listen carefully to wifely persuasion. He's a fool if he doesn't pay attention to her. What a fool David would have been if he hadn't listened to Abigail's counsel when she dissuaded him from massacring the house of Nabal (1 Samuel 25). Priscilla's name is often mentioned before her husband Aquila's name, probably because she was the more verbal of the two (Acts 18:18, 26; Romans 16:3; 2 Timothy 4:19). The excellent wife of Proverbs 31 was to her husband a fountain of wisdom (31:12, 26).

Sam Waldron's words are profound here:

> Men! Male headship is not embarrassed by the reality that a wife's character may have enormous influence, or her wisdom a great power in shaping your decisions! Do you allow yourself to be sanctified by your wife's graces and virtues? Do you permit yourself to be influenced in your decisions by the wisdom of your wife? If you do not, you are acting in a very foolish manner! If you have so cowed her that she's afraid to counsel you freely, you are the loser. Don't argue that such influence will violate your headship. Such an argument totally misunderstands what headship is!
>
> Women! Male headship is not abolished because you are smarter, or more educated or even bigger or stronger than your husband. It is not abolished by your ability to manipulate or out-argue your husband, or by your more assertive personality. All those things do not mean that your husband is not your head or that you do not need to respect him, obey him, and allow him to lead you! Male headship is not primarily a mater of brains, muscles, or personalities. It is a matter of divinely appointed leadership, which no amount of brains, muscles or personality permits you to usurp or ignore.[3]

The husband is the God-appointed head of *every* marriage.

2. Lordship

Our family once watched a movie about an African-American man who was appointed by the school board as head coach of a high school football team that for years had been ruled by a very successful white coach, who was now demoted to the status of assistant. The politically displaced assistant resented the new authority over him, and in many subtle ways attempted to intimidate the new head coach into a practical submission. Everything came to a head one day when the black coach introduced the team to a new playbook. The old plays and formations of the past decade would be discarded for the new offensive and defensive schemes designed by the new coach. The white assistant was livid and laid into the black head coach. The new coach boldly responded this way: "Look, I'm the coach. I'm not going to apologize for being here and taking charge. It's my job to run this team the way I deem best. I'm not trespassing here. I'm just doing my job."

A few years ago, I saw from my office window a man driving his tractor from the open farm field onto the back yard of my neighbor who was away vacationing. I wondered what was going on, so I ran out to talk to the man who was now beginning to mow down the waist high grass. He told me that the owner of the property had authorized him to cut and bale the two acres of land into hay. He too was just doing his job.

In both of the above cases, the men at work were aggressively carrying out their assignments. They weren't intruding or trespassing. They'd been authorized to exercise *lordship* over their respective fields of endeavor, and they were about the business of imposing their ideas and their tools on the fields.

In the beginning, man was commissioned by God to exercise a benevolent dominion over the earth and the garden (Genesis 1:28-30). He was given *lordship*, the authorization to *subdue* and *rule*. This *lordship* extends into his *marital* and *domestic* life.

> **1 Peter 3:6** *Thus Sarah obeyed Abraham, calling him lord, and you have become her children if you do what is right without being frightened by any fear.*

> **Ephesians 5:22** *Wives, be subject to your own husbands, as to the Lord.*

> **1 Timothy 3:4** *He must be one who manages (rules) his own household*

> *well, keeping his children under control with all dignity.*

This *lordship* theme is fundamentally resident in the very title of *husband*. The dictionary definition of *husband* in its archaic original is "to manage carefully."

Notice how the King James Version enlists the archaic definition:

> **Genesis 9:20** *And Noah began to be an husbandman, and he planted a vineyard:*

> **Zechariah 13:5** *But he shall say, I am no prophet, I am an husbandman; for man taught me to keep cattle from my youth.*

> **John 15:1** *I am the true vine, and my Father is the husbandman.*

It is tragic that in our culture the word *husband* is understood as nothing more than a male legally tied (for a few years) to a particular female. But as the etymology of the word should indicate, much more is involved, *Husbandry* is careful management of resources—it is stewardship. And when someone undertakes to *husband* a woman, he must understand that it cannot be done unless he acts with authority.

He must act as though *he has a right to be where he is*. He is the *lord* of the garden, and he has been commanded by God to see to it that this garden bears much fruit. This cannot be accomplished by "hanging around" in the garden and *being nice*. The garden must be managed, and ruled, and kept, and tilled. For many *husbands*, this is an alien concept.[4]

A godly husband will exercise a kind and benevolent lordship over his marriage. He'll dedicate himself to wisely and tenderly cultivating his wife and family. He'll not sit back as the sluggard couch potato passively watching his wife attempt to order the marriage and home life. He'll put his hand to the plow assertively, gently, kindly, and prudently imposing his leadership onto the field of his home.

As a pastor, I've found that this is the very kind of man that a godly woman craves. "I just wish he'd take charge of our marriage and family!" she says in frustration about her *passive* husband. In contrast, the happiest women I know are those wedded to men who boldly employ their lordship role as husband in *assertive* nurturing of their wives.

Cheryl was a very gifted and capable wife and a wonderful mother to her four very young sons. She had taken on a number of heavy "outside responsibilities" on a civic festival board, on church committees, etc. Her husband, Jeff, observed the "overload fatigue" in Cheryl's frayed emotions and physical health, and gently but firmly put his foot down: "For now, Honey, no more outside responsibilities. I think you should resign them all. At this time in your life, you've got to focus on your home and your children." At first, she wanted to run to her bedroom and cry. But then after a few minutes, she realized that her *husband* was absolutely right. Jeff's assertive pruning, though painful, was just what she needed. Since then, the domestic fruit has been sweet.

Cheryl is thankful she has a man of dominion who is her husband, and not a passive-purple four-ball. She's thankful he's willing to *intrude* his authority into her life so that she may become a fruitful field.

> **2 Chronicles 26:10** *And he (King Uzziah) built towers in the wilderness and hewed many cisterns, for he had much livestock, both in the lowland and in the plain. He also had plowmen and vinedressers in the hill country and the fertile fields, for he loved the soil* (KJV: "for he loved husbandry").

Husbands *love* your wives by assertively, attentively and gently cultivating their lives.

3. Servanthood

A biblical thinking man will view his husbanding in terms of headship and lordship. But make no mistake. These scriptural principles provide no green light for a harsh or abrasive tyranny. To the contrary, biblical husbanding must be carried out in the spirit of *servanthood.*

Consider King Uzziah above who "loved the soil". This deep fondness and affection for the land drove him to pour out sweat and expensive resources for its fruitfulness. He built towers for the land's protection against crop stealing marauders. He dug the cisterns for the soil's irrigation and livestock population. He hired the plowmen and vinedressers for its cultivation. He spent a fortune of time and gold on his land "because he loved the soil."

Many old farmers will tell you that they have a *love affair* with the land they farm. They nurture it with fertilizer. They comb it with their tiller. They spray it with their special recipes. They sweat over it with their own perspiration. They bleed over it. They become obsessed with the weather patterns above it. They lose sleep over it. They pray for the prosperity of it. They selflessly serve their land. Likewise, a biblical husband will serve his wife.

Of course, the Lord Jesus is the model husband.

> **Ephesians 5:25-27** *Husbands, love your wives, just as Christ also loved the church and gave Himself up for her; 26 that He might sanctify her, having cleansed her by the washing of water with the word, 27 that He might present to Himself the church in all her glory, having no spot or wrinkle or any such thing; but that she should be holy and blameless.*

Yes, He is the Head and Lord of His Bride. But these crucial roles were exercised with the tenderest of self-sacrificial love. Did our Savior come down to his earthly bride and recline on a sofa, expecting her to fetch His slippers and newspaper? To the contrary, He came and *emptied* Himself out for her good.

> **Mark 10:45** *For even the Son of Man did not come to be served, but to serve, and to give His life a ransom for many.*

For His Bride, He left heaven's glory. For His Bride, He was willing to wiggle in Bethlehem's manger and work in Nazareth's workshop. For His Bride, he was numbered with the transgressors in His baptism. For His Bride, He endured near starvation and Satanic temptation in the wilderness. For His Bride, He absorbed years of public ministry abuse by a wicked and adulterous generation. For His Bride, he had no place to lay his head. For His bride, he marched fearlessly toward the Jerusalem slaughterhouse. For His Bride, He broke the bread in the upper room. For His Bride, He was drenched in blood-like sweat. For His Bride, He said, "Not my will, but Thine be done." For His Bride, He handed Himself over to a kangaroo court. For His Bride, He was again and again spat upon and struck in the head. For His Bride, he stood barebacked at a pillar-absorbing scourge after scourge. For His Bride, he was mocked while holding a reed scepter. For His Bride, He carried and collapsed under the crossbeam. For His Bride, He was stripped naked. For His Bride, He absorbed the spikes into His hands and feet. For His Bride, he was lifted up between heaven and earth as an accursed spectacle. For His Bride, He hung before head wagging scoffers. For His Bride, he gasped for breath and cried out "My God, My God, why hast Thou forsaken me?" For His Bride, He finished it—and died.

This is an overwhelming model for husbands. We wouldn't have dared to put it before ourselves. We would have considered it profanity to join together two things so far apart: *sinful men* and the *sinless Savior*! But with this very ideal, the Holy Spirit has charged us.

D. Martyn Lloyd-Jones asks:

> How many of us have realized that we are always to think of the married state in terms of the doctrine of the atonement?[5]

I must tend to her with an attitude of *self-sacrifice.* I can't be content to sit back and observe with appreciation her selflessness toward me, as she rises early, labors long, and works late into the night for my family. I've been given the charge of sacrificing myself for her good. I've got to *lead her* instead of *being mothered by her.* I've got to *serve her* instead of being satisfied with *being served by her.* I need to beat down my love of leisure and my right to watch the NCAA Basketball Tournament. What about her and the benefit she'd receive from a couple of solid hours away from the children? I need to assertively *subdue* and *rule* in the lives of those children instead of acting as a passive spectator to her mothering. I've got to take the initiative to romance her, pray with her, and complete her "honey-do" lists. I need to make the advancement of her personal and spiritual prosperity the chief project of my earthly life.

I recently asked the women in our church to recount the most romantic thing your husband has ever done for you. Here's a sampling:

Heidi tearfully told about Andy's encouraging her to train for and run a Five Kilometer race before she turned thirty. "All summer he pushed me to get out and run, even when I didn't want to. On race day, Andy (an accomplished runner himself), ran alongside Heidi the whole way. I didn't realize this until after the race when someone told me that during the last quarter of a mile, Andy had dropped way back so that the gathered crowd wouldn't feel sorry for me, being the last one to finish. Andy took last place for me!"

Pam told about Joe's driving her to an unexpected location: "Where are we going?" she questioned. Joe smiled and told Pam that she could relax for the next few days because the kids were all taken care of, the household responsibilities were covered, her bags were packed in the trunk, and the two of them were heading for a bed and breakfast get-a-way. Joe chimed in: "Yeah, right then she started to cry. I thought I'd blown it!" Pam reported: "Just the fact that he'd *planned all of this out beforehand*, just for me, overwhelmed me."

Debbie reported: "Jon is not the traditional romantic type. He shows his love to me in other ways. He works very hard. He wants to come home to us. He is very conscientious about taking care of the van. He's been remodeling the basement. When I need to drive somewhere, he's always ready with directions so that I know exactly where I'm going. When he needs to return equipment back to town, he often waits till the younger children are in bed so that the two of us can go together and stop for coffee on the way home. Jon shows he loves me in hands-on ways, as opposed to the traditional candy and flowers."

Sharon wrote her response:

Pr. Mark,

Well I thought of two things, one very short, so I will give you both of them!

1. One day after we had had an "argument," Ray came home from work with a flower in a styrofoam cup; he had pulled over to the side of the road and picked a flower, and put it in a cup of water to bring home to me. It stands above the many flowers and roses that he has given me. Although it didn't cost any money and may have looked "cheap" to some, it was a precious, heartfelt gift to me.

2. As I told you on the phone, one of the best and most romantic things in my mind was when Ray cleaned my entire house when Blake was born; when I came home from the hospital, it was spotlessly clean. He had waxed the floors, did the windows, cleaned the kitchen and bathrooms, did the laundry, it was amazing! We lived in California at the time, in the military, and far away from any family that might have come to help. It might not sound "romantic" in most people's minds, but I knew that to do this, he had to spend time doing things he did NOT like to do, and he did it just for ME, because he knew I could relax better in a clean house. A true act of self-sacrifice for someone else's well being - that's romance!!

This was a hard question because there are so many things Ray does, maybe not the classic romantic acts in the world's view, but he shows that

> *he loves me by countless everyday things. Going to work and working hard, supporting a big family and considering it a blessing and not a curse to do so; always kissing me "hello" when he comes home and "goodbye" when he leaves, etc, etc! I could go on, but I won't!*
>
> *Well, you asked for it! That's my sermon! :)*
>
> *Sharon*

Sharon, by the way, gracefully mothers eight children, spanning the ages of five to twenty. She's a highly respected woman who loves her challenging and energy draining vocation as a homemaker. She thrives under the care of her conscientious *husband.*

> It is said that the glowworm never shines after it has become a parent. Some women lose the luster of all delicacy and refinement under the influence of men whom they call their *husbands.* The aim of the true husband should be to make the character of the wife a *glorious* character, "without spot or blemish."[6]

As a Christ-like husband, I must serve my wife with Golgotha love. That means I must lay down my life for her not only when I'm inclined to and when she's loveable, but *especially* when it's excruciatingly painful, when I'm disinclined, and she's very unlovable — just as the Lord Jesus loves His bride.

Being a four-ball won't get it done.

1 Nashville: Thomas Nelson Publishers, 1987, pp.7,65
2 Philipsburg, NJ: Presbyterian and Reformed, 1985, p.14
3 *The Role of Women in the Church* (Grand Rapids: Truth For Eternity Ministries, 1996), p.4
4 Douglas Wilson, *Reforming Marriage* (Moscow, ID: Canon Press, 1995), p.77
5 D. Martin Lloyd-Jones, *Life in the Spirit, An Exposition of Ephesians 5:18 to 6:9* (Grand Rapids: Baker Book House, 1976), pp.130ff.
6 D. Thomas, *Pulpit Commentary: Ephesians, Vol.20* (Peabody, MA: Hendrickson), p.48

Chapter 21
Assertive Talking

Somewhere an author wrote about the need for men to love their wives as Christ loved the church, and for men to nourish and cherish their wives as Christ does the church (Ephesians 5:25-29). He put it very bluntly: "Staring at the idiot box until it's time for sex is not one of God's appointed means for doing so." That would be the four-ball approach.

Every married man must take a very serious and aggressive approach to his husbanding. He's got to make the field of his marriage a high-priority site for the exercise of manly dominion. Most farmers will tell you that their *plow* is the most important tool in their sheds when it comes to preparing and cultivating their soil. Without using that plow, farming is a pretty futile endeavor.

In the field of marriage, the most important tool of the domestic husbandman is his mouth. With his mouth a man speaks words. With his words, he cultivates the mind, emotions, and soul of his precious wife. Unfortunately, the mouths of many men are collecting dust instead of turning soil. The lives of many women have become barren wildernesses because they've been neglected by uncommunicative husbands; men who indulge themselves in selfish silence, men who are stingy with their words, men whose typical answer is one of *no comment*, men who like Adam in the snake infested garden leave it to their wives to do the talking.

Generally speaking, females are the more verbal gender; the chatter level at a typical baby shower is usually much more intense than in typical hunting blind. While working at a golf country club as a teen, I noted much more player conversation on Ladies' Day than on Doctor's Day. I recently read a study that attempted to compare the number of words per day spoken by women in contrast to men. Women overwhelmingly out talked the men!

I've been intrigued with the insightful distinctions made in the Scriptures related to peculiar gender related besetting sins. For instance, Jesus says:

> **Matthew 5:27** *You have heard that it was said, 'YOU SHALL NOT COMMIT ADULTERY'; 28 but I say to you, that everyone who looks on a woman to lust for her has committed adultery with her already in his heart.*

Lusting is more of a besetting sin for the male gender. But *gossiping* is more of a besetting sin for the female gender:

> **1 Timothy 5:13** *And at the same time they (widows) also learn to be idle, as they go around from house to house; and not merely idle, but also gossips and busybodies, talking about things not proper to mention.*

> **Titus 2:3** *Older women likewise are to be reverent in their behavior, not malicious gossips, nor enslaved to much wine, teaching what is good,*

Even the Bible recognizes that women tend to speak more fluidly and easily than do men. And because of this they need to set a special guard over their mouths. But simply because males are not typically the spontaneous communicators that females are, does not let men off the hook.

Lou Priolo, in his book *The Complete Husband*, quotes a typical husband who finds conversation with his wife to be tedious.

> But the truth is, I don't really enjoy talking to my wife, especially at night when I'm tired after having talked all day! I usually talk for one reason—*because I have to*. Communication is a means to an end for me: the means of accomplishing some task. For my wife, communication seems to be a means *in and of itself*. I don't get it, and I certainly don't enjoy it![1]

But the truth is, that we're not to live by our *inclinations*, but by biblical *instructions*. We're solemnly bound and obligated to love our wives as Christ loved his bride, the church. A river of words pouring out of His mouth marked Christ's ministry to His bride. In the Gospels, we read the eloquent Sermon on the Mount (Matthew 5-7), His spellbinding parables, the prophetic Olivet Discourse (Matthew 24-25), His crucifixion eve "Upper Room Discourse" (John 13-17) and the "Road to Emmaus" monologue (Luke 24:25-27). Observe carefully how the perfect Man related to His dear bride. He tenderly cultivated her with the words of His mouth. He was a *big talker*, a willing communicator. He painstakingly revealed Himself to His bride. As her heavenly Intercessor, He patiently listens to her needs and concerns. He provides wise input for her every concern.

Proverbs 2:6 *For the LORD gives wisdom; From His mouth come knowledge and understanding.*

Proverbs 10:31 *The mouth of the righteous flows with wisdom...*

A Christ-like husband will assertively enlist his mouth in manfully taking up the role of wonderful counselor (Isaiah 9:6) to his bride. But the Christ-like husband won't only be a teacher of wisdom; he'll also be a revealer of himself. He'll be willing to "open up" to his wife, by disclosing to her many secrets of his heart.

Since marriage (becoming "one flesh") is the most intimate of personal relationships, the revelation of yourself to your spouse should exceed the revelation of yourself to any other person (except the Lord, who knows you more intimately than you know yourself; cf. Ps. 139:1-6). Practically speaking, that means you should be more intimate with, and reveal more of yourself to, your spouse than your closest friend, your parents or your children.

We read in Genesis 2:24-25, "For this cause a man shall leave his father and his mother, and shall cleave to his wife; and they shall become one flesh. And the man and his wife were both naked and were not ashamed." Adam and Eve's *nakedness* speaks not primarily of their lack of clothing, but rather of the total openness and frankness that they enjoyed with one another before sin entered into their lives. It's our sin (especially the sin of pride) that keeps us from being as candid and straightforward as were Adam and Eve before the fall. It's God's intention for Christian husbands and wives to increasingly become more and more *naked and unashamed* with each other, as were our first parents in the Garden of Eden."[2]

So, men, we've got to overcome our passive-purple-four-ball reluctance to communicate. We've got to make a conscientious effort to become God-like in our verbal interaction. As God made it a habit in Eden to have "cool of the day" discussions with His dear ones (Genesis 3:8f), so should we with our dear wives.

Think of it. Next time the house is quiet and you usually go down the basement to tinker in your workshop, read your newspaper or watch a baseball game, this time do something different: Consciously choose to sit down on the sofa next to your wife while she's faithfully folding the laundry. There you ask her, "So, how was your day?" or "What have you been thinking about?" or "How are you feeling?" Though she might faint from shock the first time, you'll eventually find these "cool of the day" interactions to be very fruitful and God honoring.

May God help us to be *men of dominion* who throw off *passive* silence and put on *assertive* talking.

21 / ASSERTIVE TALKING

1 Lou Priolo, *The Complete Husband* (Amityville, NY: Calvary Press, 1999), pp.48-49
2 Ibid., pp.47-48

Chapter 22
Atmosphere Setting

I know of certain men who are very meticulous about exercising careful dominion over the household thermostat. I'm one of them. It's a matter of stewardship, right? During the winter, we want the house not too warm, so as to waste money, but not too chilly so as to promote cold feet, sore throats and runny noses. At night and when we leave the house, the thermostat must be turned way down. During the summer, the air conditioner is used sparingly, but avoiding a sweaty night's sleep is a priority. Yes, many of us men are convinced that the physical temperature of the home must be fastidiously monitored and conscientiously set.

But what about the relational temperature of our homes? Many of us who are conscientiously fastidious about *setting* the physical temperature, passively neglect the relational temperature. We may, to our shame, often permit extended seasons of scorching hot irritation to continue on in our relationships with our wives. Icy cold periods of alienation can be allowed to extend out day after day after day.

Late one December afternoon, I announced to my wife that I was heading off to the electronics store to purchase the family computer we'd decided on as a Christmas gift for the children. I also told her that I was taking along our firstborn son in order I might instruct him in the art of *purchase negotion* or *dickering*. Prudent aggressiveness can save you hundreds of dollars in such a transaction. I thought taking along a student was a high priority. But Dianne didn't. For her, maintaining the Christmas surprise element was a priority. I was looking at it *practically*. She was looking at it *sentimentally*. We exchanged harsh words. I overruled her opinion, and when we left for the store, she wasn't happy.

When we returned, I was able to report to Dianne how the store had tried to pull a "bait and switch" technique on us, thinking we'd pay hundreds of dollars more for another machine. I asked to speak with the manager, who upon hearing my complaint, apologized and agreed to give me the higher priced computer at the lower price and even threw in, free of charge, some additional items. I was thrilled that Jared had been there to witness the educational drama. But Dianne wasn't thrilled. She was irritated with me because I had trampled her. But I was convinced that I had been in the right, and I let an icy cold alienation between the two of us go on day after day after day.

I was acting like a *passive-purple-four-ball.* I wasn't actively *setting* the temperature and atmosphere of my marriage.

In situations like this, we've got to act like men of dominion. We've got to grab the dial of our marriage, take the relationship in hand, and lovingly *subdue* it to the glory of God. For me, it involves tenderly approaching my wife and asking her to talk about the point of controversy. This usually involves retiring to our bedroom, closing the door and discussing through the variables related to our conflict. By the grace of God, this typically results in confessions of poor judgment or sin, followed by an expression of plans for repentance, and oftentimes a somewhat warm embrace. The return of heat isn't always instant! But at least by aggressive subduing, the thermostat has been properly set. Inevitably, the marriage temperature becomes pleasantly comfortable again.

Douglas Wilson's book *Reforming Marriage* is excellent in addressing the necessity of a man's *subduing* the relational atmosphere of his marriage and home:

> How would you describe the spiritual aroma of your home? When visitors arrive, before virtually anything is said or done, what is one of the first things they notice about your family? In many cases, it is the *aroma.* Do they feel as though a bad attitude crawled under your refrigerator and died? Or do they think someone has been baking spiritual bread in the kitchen all afternoon? . . . John Bunyan once exhorted husbands to be "such a believing husband to your believing wife that she may say, 'God has not only given me a husband, but such a husband as preaches to me every day the way of Christ to His church.'" The health of all other

> relationships in the home depends upon the health of this relationship, and the key is found in how the husband is treating his wife. Or, put in another way, when mamma ain't happy, ain't nobody happy.
>
> When sins are confessed, it's like picking something up that was dropped on the carpet. If a person learns to pick things up immediately, a thousand things can be dropped on the carpet, and the home will still remain clean. But if things are only picked up once every six months, the result will be an overwhelming house-cleaning job. To continue the illustration, some homes are so messed up, that those responsible for cleaning simply do not know where to start. They do not necessarily like the way it is, but they are simply overwhelmed. But such things always accumulate *one at a time.* If they had been picked up as fast as they'd been dropped, then the home would have remained clean.
>
> In the same way, "things" need to be picked up in all relationships. Confession of wrongdoing should always occur *immediately*. "He who covers his sins will not prosper. But whoever confesses and forsakes them will have mercy" (Prov. 28:13). Nothing good will ever be accomplished through postponement of confession. . . .
>
> . . . Suppose a man comes home from work and his wife cheerfully greets him. He had a bad day, so he snaps at her and stomps off into the living room. He reads the paper, glowering for ten minutes. At that point, he cannot calm down, walk into the kitchen and say, "Hi, hon, what's for dinner?" He cannot act as though nothing happened. His sin affects the joy of the relationship. The *fact* of their relationship is not affected—they are still husband and wife—but the quality of it *is* affected. There can be no genuine fellowship between them until that sin is addressed.[1]

For a godly man, relational passivity simply must not be an option.

On more than one occasion I've sat reading in my chair alongside our bed while my wife has *coolly* prepared for the night. I say *coolly*, because she wasn't warm. She wasn't warm because we'd had a relationship-breaching squabble. Now I know that I've got to do something about this before we go to sleep. I know that the man who fails to grab hold of and *subdue* the relational atmosphere of his marriage before the lights go out is leaving the front door wide open all night for a lion to slip in and make his home.

> **Ephesians 4:26-27** *BE ANGRY, AND yet DO NOT SIN; do not let the sun go down on your anger, 27 and do not give the devil an opportunity.*

Stuart Olyott comments on these verses:

> We are not to go to bed and brood. (Even) righteous anger, like the manna from heaven, breeds worms if it is kept overnight. There are too many worms to count — bitterness, revenge, malice, spite, an unforgiving spirit, sharpness, grudges, hostility, and irritability . . . the list could to on and on. We are to wake each morning with no feelings of hurt *at all* carried over from the day before. If not, we shall be in a situation that the devil will definitely exploit. Unchristlikeness and unbrotherliness will take up residence in our hearts, and who knows where that will lead? No Christian is ever to let this happen, says the inspired apostle.[2]

But I don't *feel* like reconciling right now. It's late. I'm tired. Besides, if she feels the sting of alienation for a little longer, she might come around to my way of thinking. More than once I've shamefully done this.

But I can't keep passively reading. I've got to stand up like a man. I'm solemnly commissioned by my Lord to grab hold of the reigns of my straying marriage and *subdue* it by restoring it back to a narrow road course. Even if she says that she doesn't want to talk about it right now, I must insist on our refusing to retire without reconciliation. It may take the better part of an hour, sometimes much more. But we've got to be able to sincerely pray together as two souls reconciled to one another bringing an acceptable sacrifice to God.

This kind of assertive marital "atmosphere setting" brings a sweet aroma to the whole household. Instead of permitting the carcasses to rot under the refrigerator, a man of dominion will get up, exert himself in removing that refrigerator out of its filthy slot, and thoroughly clean up the mess underneath. Then usually, by God's grace, he's able to sit back and enjoy the aroma of her baked sweet bread wafting through the house.

Four-ballism, on the other hand, stinks.

22 / ATMOSPHERE SETTING

1 Douglas Wilson, *Reforming Marriage* (Moscow, ID: Canon Press, 1995), pp.7-8; 66-67

2 Stuart Olycott, *Alive in Christ* (Darlington, UK: Evangelical Press, 1994), pp.110-111

Chapter 23
Responsibility Assuming

When I speak of *responsibility assuming* in marriage, I'm not talking about a man's need to step up and take care of those honey-do-lists like the one I recently saw on the kitchen refrigerator:

1. Repair Van Blinker (so she wouldn't get tail ended)
2. Purchase New Gas Grill (so we could have flame broiled burgers)
3. Clean and Install Screens (so we could get fresh air into the house)

Responsible exercising of dominion over these tasks is basic to any man's household headship. But I'm focusing here on a more grand issue. A husband must assume *responsibility for the course of the marriage as a whole.*

In March of 1989, the Exxon Valdez oil tanker struck a reef in Prince William Sound in southern Alaska causing one of the worst oil spills in history. More than ten million gallons of spilled oil polluted many miles of the coast, killing thousands of birds, fish and mammals. The cleanup cost was astronomical. An uncertified officer was at the helm when the tanker slammed into that reef. But rightly so, it was *the captain* who was charged, prosecuted, and convicted of criminal conduct for the mishap. Why? Because his rank of captain forced him to *assume responsibility* for every activity that occurred aboard that ship. Though his first mate may have erred in poorly navigating the coastline, the captain was ultimately responsible for the straying course.

Likewise, I often sit before couples whose marriages are straying for one reason or another. There may be a generally bad aroma in the relationship. The wife may be bitter and spiteful toward her husband. It may be obvious that she's got plenty of repenting to do. But inevitably, I turn to the husband and say, "Now you realize that you're the one who's primarily responsible for this mess!" His expression may be one of dumbfounded disbelief, to which I'll continue, "Sure, there are privileges involved in headship, but there are also painful liabilities. You're *the captain* of this marriage, and you're the one who's let it stray onto this bad course."

"You da man!" I tell him, referring to the Genesis 3 account when Eve's foolish deliberating with the serpent issued in history's worst shipwreck. Who did the Lord come looking for? *The captain*!

> **Genesis 3:8-9** *And they heard the sound of the LORD God walking in the garden in the cool of the day, and the man and his wife hid themselves from the presence of the LORD God among the trees of the garden. 9 Then the LORD God called to the man, and said to him, "Where are you?"*

I'm not saying Eve was without guilt; nor am I saying that a bitter wife is without guilt. I'm simply saying that the man must be *responsibility assuming* in his posture. He is the *chief cause for the mess*, and he is the *chief custodian* for the cleanup.

I once spent an evening counseling with Bruce and Michelle. Michelle reported the numerous relational difficulties she was having with Kirsten, Bruce's biological teenage daughter from his first marriage. They just weren't getting along. Female catfights were almost daily affairs. Kirsten resented Michelle's intrusion into her father's life, while Michelle resented Kirsten's attempts to remain *the most important woman* in Bruce's life. Bruce appeared to be cruising above it all, until I turned to him and assured him that the chaos was primarily his fault! He needed to assume chief responsibility by aggressively subduing and ruling in this matter. He needed to, in no uncertain terms, *instruct* his daughter on the biblical framework of this new household. Dad has become one flesh with Michelle. This marriage union is the *hub* of the new family. Kirsten is only a *spoke*, and will only find joy, happiness, and the smile of God in assuming her God-ordained position as subordinate daughter. Bruce needed to tangibly express his chief allegiance to his wife, back her up in her motherly authority, and reaffirm his secondary fatherly affection for his daughter. When Bruce began his *responsibility assuming*, the course of the family ship naturally began to right itself.

But *responsibility assuming* isn't the natural response of sinful men. Instead, when we arrive home after a long day of hard work and encounter marital and domestic strife, we're natively inclined to find a secluded hammock in a distant cabin of the ship. One man I know used to make a beeline for the bathroom where he'd read the newspaper behind a locked door for the better part of an hour!

Men, we don't have the luxury of retreating to such *boyish hideouts.* We've got to assume our position *at the helm* of our marriages. We've been called to *subdue* and *rule.* We are heads, captains, *and managers.*

> **1 Timothy 3:4-5** *He (an overseer, pastor) must be one who manages his own household well, keeping his children under control with all dignity 5 (but if a man does not know how to manage his own household, how will he take care of the church of God?)...*

> **1 Timothy 3:12** *Let deacons be husbands of only one wife, and good managers of their children and their own households.*

All men are to *manage* their households. Those qualified as pastors and deacons are to do it peculiarly well. Lou Priolo puts it well:

> When there are conflicts in his household, a good manager sees to it that they're resolved scripturally. When there are conflicts in his home, he sees to it that they're resolved biblically. He helps with the coordination of scheduling. He sees to it that everyone in his household is treated with justice and equity. Additionally, should someone be temporarily unable to pull his or her load, he is willing to roll up his sleeves and "pinch hit" for one of his incapacitated team members. Simply put, a good manager is willing to do such things that may not fall within his usual responsibilities, such as changing diapers, fixing meals, vacuuming floors, or going grocery shopping.[1]

For some men, this headship responsibility is very difficult to live out. In some marriages, it's the wife who "wears the pants." She may even somewhat prefer that he passively retreat to his boyish tree house. This upside down dynamic was forecasted as a dimension of the curse.

> **Genesis 3:16** *To the woman He said, "I will greatly multiply Your pain in childbirth, In pain you shall bring forth children; Yet your desire shall be for your husband, And he shall rule over you."*

I believe the gist of the passage is: "your desire will be to control your husband, but he shall rule over you." In other words, as a result of the fall, a woman's inclination is to control her husband. But God has said that the husband is to *manage* or rule his wife (not domineeringly or dictatorially, but sacrificially and lovingly).

So when a young mother's vitamin selling cottage industry has for the one hundredth time made a shambles of the household because it's again caused her to neglect her priority duties, it may be time for the husband to act. He may gently, but firmly, take his stand at the helm and announce to her that it's time to pull the plug on the vitamin business.

When the end of the month financial reckonings show that the family is falling steadily behind, the man of the house may need to put his foot down with his chief purchasing officer by saying: "Now honey, I've made these rigid budget categories, and we've got to religiously stick to them whether we like it or not!"

When a spirit of bitterness or contentiousness persists for days, he may need to step in and say: "Honey, let's go to the bedroom and talk about this conflict. Our continuing on in this course of sinful strife is not an option before God."

And remember men, more often it's we who need to be subdued, not our wives, and rebuked by the Word of God. The next chapter will address more fully this solemn personal duty.

Instead of being *passive-purple-four-balls*, let's be *responsibility-assuming* men of dominion.

23 / RESPONSIBILITY ASSUMING

1 *The Complete Husband*, p.219

Chapter 24
Sin Mortifying

Peter the Great made a law in 1722 that if any nobleman beat or mistreated his slaves he should be looked upon as insane, and a guardian should be appointed to take care of his person and his estate. Subsequently, this great king once struck his gardener who was in actuality a very honorable man. The gardener took to his bed and died a few days later. Peter, hearing of this, exclaimed with tears in his eyes, "Alas! I've civilized my own subjects; I have conquered other nations; yet have I not been able to civilize or conquer myself."

Yes, as men, we're called to *subdue* and *rule* in our vocations, in our households, and in our marriages. But first and foremost we're called to *subdue* and *rule* ourselves.

> **Proverbs 25:28** *Like a city that is broken into and without walls is a man who has no control over his spirit.*

Our attempts to manage our family will be doomed to failure if we're not making sincere headway in our endeavors to subdue and rule over our own passions. I just returned home from a counseling session with a young husband and wife who, about a year and a half ago, were both saved when their near divorce brought them to their wit's end and to the foot of the cross. Their marriage has made wonderful progress in the last eighteen months, but they've reached a discouraging standstill season. As I probed for answers, the husband confided that his smoking habit haunted him. "Every time I smoke, I know I'm breaking the sixth commandment. I'm harming my body. My wife knows I'm violating my conscience. Even my three-year old son knows I'm sinning." He knew that he was sabotaging his marital and parental headship by failing to *subdue* and *rule* over his own passions and appetites.

He was right. We severely cripple our management leverage by our failure to manage ourselves. When we fail to take a bit and bridle to our own passions, our dominion endeavors appear hypocritical and hollow.

If I don't reign in my anger, I'll not have much success winning over my wife. If I can't trample down my pride, I'll not be able to have her conscience. If I selfishly indulge myself, I won't constrain her to selflessly serve. If I quietly pout, I can't convince her to openly love.

On the upside, a wife who views her husband ruling over his own spirit, putting to death his pride, beating down his laziness, and overcoming his reticence to communicate, will be motivated to reciprocate in kind. Great respect and esteem is built up by the man whose wife sees him daily yanking himself out of bed early enough to have his personal devotions, habitually refusing that extra dessert in order to avoid a beer belly, and consistently denying himself in finishing off irksome home improvement projects.

Nothing undermines a marriage more than a husband's failure to *subdue* and *rule* over his own sexual passions. Her observing his roving eyes seeking a glance of a pretty jogger out of his rear view mirror erodes a wife's confidence in her husband.

> **Job 31:1** *"I have made a covenant with my eyes; How then could I gaze at a virgin?*

> **Proverbs 4:25-27** *Let your eyes look directly ahead, And let your gaze be fixed straight in front of you. 26 Watch the path of your feet, And all your ways will be established. 27 Do not turn to the right nor to the left; Turn your foot from evil.*

> **Matthew 5:28-29** *but I say to you, that everyone who looks on a woman to lust for her has committed adultery with her already in his heart. 29And if your right eye makes you stumble, tear it out, and throw it from you; for it is better for you that one of the parts of your body perish, than for your whole body to be thrown into hell.*

A wife's admiration for her husband is seriously damaged when she finds him watching impurity on the television. I've heard women give sighs of deep disappointment.

> **Psalm 101:2b-3a** *I will walk within my house in the integrity of my heart. 3 I will set no worthless thing before my eyes;*

Her respect for her husband is nearly devastated when using the Internet, she stumbles over his "cookie history" that reveals a sordid pattern of visiting pornographic websites. In her eyes, his integrity is brought to *utter ruin.*

> **Proverbs 5:1ff** *My son, give attention to my wisdom, Incline your ear to my understanding; . . . 3 For the lips of an adulteress drip honey, And smoother than oil is her speech; . . . 8 Keep your way far from her, And do not go near the door of her house, 9 Lest you give your vigor to others, And your years to the cruel one; . . . 12 And you say, "How I have hated instruction! And my heart spurned reproof! 13 "And I have not listened to the voice of my teachers, Nor inclined my ear to my instructors! 14 "I was almost in utter ruin In the midst of the assembly and congregation."*

I remember when a former President's sexual immorality was headline news. The liberal media rushed to soften the blow of this disgrace by claiming that ninety-eight percent of married men have been sexually unfaithful just like the President, and that the two percent who deny having been unfaithful were liars. The assertion was, "Hey, we all do it. What's the big deal?"

That assertion is a lie from the pit. We don't all do it! Christian men of God don't do it! Christ's disciples are mighty men who are given grace to exercise dominion over their sexual lives, to *subdue* and *rule* over their sexual passions, to put to death the impure deeds of the flesh. Though the beast of Revelation 16 may get his damning mark on the foreheads (habitual thinking) and hands (habitual behavior) of countless millions in this wicked and adulterous generation (Revelation 13:16-18), not so with the remnant of the saints.

> **Revelation 14:1,4** *And I looked, and behold, the Lamb was standing on Mount Zion, and with Him one hundred and forty-four thousand, having His name and the name of His Father written on their foreheads. . . . 4 These are the ones who have not been defiled with women, for they have*

> *kept themselves chaste. These are the ones who follow the Lamb wherever He goes. These have been purchased from among men as first fruits to God and to the Lamb.*

Gentlemen, this must be our pattern of life. One great means of keeping ourselves from being defiled by women is by each of us keeping ourselves exhilarated with our own wives.

> **Proverbs 5:15-19** *Drink water from your own cistern, And fresh water from your own well. 16 Should your springs be dispersed abroad, Streams of water in the streets? 17 Let them be yours alone, And not for strangers with you. 18 Let your fountain be blessed, And rejoice in the wife of your youth. 19 As a loving hind and a graceful doe, Let her breasts satisfy you at all times; Be exhilarated always with her love.*

The man, who's learned to play classical masterpieces on his grand piano, isn't easily distracted by every colorful harmonica or kazoo he passes by in the Vanity Fair carnival.

May the Lord keep us from the plague of four-ball passivity, and help us to aggressively slay our own sins.

Manly Dominion in Child Rearing

When I awoke yesterday to a March Monday morning, I saw that the thermometer out on our back deck read frigid minus two degrees. I'd heard that the ice formations on Lake Michigan were spectacular this year, so when evening approached my youngest son and I bundled up and headed off to the lakeshore. I picked up four more little boys on the way, and as dusk was approaching, we all stood high atop the sand dune overlooking the eerie sight of the frozen beach. The golden summer sand had become arctic tundra. The breaking waves had become petrified barriers. For nearly a quarter of a mile out, the lake had become a jagged obstacle course. Then, beyond the final shelf of twenty-foot high icebergs, formed by the crashing surf, was an immediate cliff drop-off, into waters that were icy and dark. The sight was spectacular! This would be a great time! What fun! My thrilled, gleeful shouting and laughing stirred up the boys.

Then, like Churchill Downs, the five boys bolted down the dune toward the lake, across the beach onto the formations. Their widening distance from me was making them look like specks in my vision. I boyishly laughed again at their excitement, sharing in their exhilaration, until I realized who I was. "I'm not a boy anymore. I am the parent figure. There's danger down there. They're drawn to that iceberg precipice like pigs drawn to the mud, and if one of them slips over the edge into water, they're dead."

Realization of my parental identity immediately sobered me up. I stopped laughing—and started shouting: "Everybody stop right where you are! Stop! Don't take another step! Don't move!" If ever there was a time for *manly dominion*, for *subduing* and *ruling*, it was right then!

That lakeshore drama well captures the effect of parenthood on an adult's life. Even unbelieving pagans, when holding for the first time their newborn child in a birthing room, are slapped sober with the new reality: "I'm not a kid anymore. This is my child! He's depending on me! I'm a Dad now! I've got to get my life together."

On a number of occasions, young parents have told me that the prod that God used to spur them out of their spiritual listlessness was the awful realization that they were no longer boys and girls; now they were fathers and mothers. This slapped them sober. They repented and got their lives in order.

When thinking of dominion, possibly the most mind-sobering sphere of all, is the sphere of child rearing. Our own flesh and blood is depending on us to responsibly *subdue* and *rule*.

Chapter 25
Manly Dominion in Child Rearing: Our Sacred Commission

I know that we can sometimes look on a birth as a rather mundane affair. Many hospitals average over a dozen births per day. Especially in our throw away age of abortion on demand, we can fail to rightly weigh the staggering significance of the conception of a new life. But in reproduction, through the instrumentality of a father and a mother, there is mysteriously brought forth from nothing, a sacred human soul. This reproductive activity is a staggering power God has *not* given to angels. We should marvel to be so blessed with the ability to produce offspring, to propagate rational and immortal spirits. Think of it! As a man at his grill ignites a stick match, so a man with his wife kindles an immortal flame—not of temporary, but of eternal duration.

> **Ecclesiastes 3:11a** *He has made everything appropriate in its time. He has also set eternity in their heart…*

It is the mysterious propagation of a rational soul that fills the reflecting soul with awe. The parent looks upon the tender face which answers to his caress with an infantile smile; he should see beneath that smile an immortal spark which he has kindled, but can never quench.

It must grow, for weal or for woe; it cannot be arrested. Just now it was not. The parents have mysteriously brought it from darkness and nothing. There is now power beneath God's throne that can remand it back to nothing, should existence prove a curse. Yes, the parents have lighted an everlasting lamp, which must burn on when the sun shall have been turned into darkness and the moon into blood, either with the glory of heaven or the lurid flame of despair.[1]

Now dear parent, look into the eyes of your children. Not only have you passed on to them *eternity*; you've also passed on to them *depravity* (a sinful nature).

> **Psalm 51:5** *Behold, I was brought forth in iniquity, And in sin my mother conceived me.*

As parents, we've been God's instrument in passing on to them not only life, but also *death*. We've passed on to them the guilt and pollution of our father Adam's sin. Through us they've been *poisoned* with a moral disease that dooms them to eternal death.

Napoleon was a ruthless and harsh dictator. While dying of agonizing stomach cancer, he gave to his Italian physician this dying command: "Return to Italy. Visit my son, and watch over his health and endeavor by every resource of your art to ward off this dire inheritance of his father's disease." Now if this evil tyrant was so earnestly compassionate toward his child, how could we fail to exhaust all means to bring our children to the *Great Physician* of souls in order to save them from the very disease with which we've *poisoned* them?

Surely, if your child scraped his knee, you'd wash it out. If he'd gashed his head, you'd apply the antiseptic and give the hug. If a viper had bitten her, you'd tie the tourniquet and suck out the poison. And having been bitten by the old serpent, will you be negligent in diligently carrying your children to Christ and making them submit to His remedies and prescriptions?

Look at that little face that gazes up at you with a smile. You parent, and in particular, you Father, have been solemnly commissioned by God as the ultimate guardian of that soul!

> **Ephesians 6:4** *And, <u>fathers</u>, do not provoke your children to anger; but <u>bring them up in the discipline and instruction of the Lord.</u>*

Notice how it doesn't say, "Pastors, bring them up in the discipline and instruction of the Lord." Nor does it say youth pastors, teachers, or even mothers; it says *fathers*. Again, the buck stops with the man of the house. The *captain* must give an account for each child on board and for every passenger entrusted to his care.

Contrary to the politically correct social engineers of our day, a father is not to passively sit back and respect the dignity of each child by letting him choose for himself a religion or belief system that's right for him. Instead, a godly father will strive to authoritatively instruct and assertively indoctrinate each of his children according to the sacred Word of God.

Regarding Abraham, the Lord said:

> **Genesis 18:19a** *"For I have chosen him, in order that he may <u>command his children and his household after him to keep the way of the LORD</u> by doing righteousness and justice;*

I recently spoke with a father who lamented to me that his teenage son refused to get up on Sunday mornings to attend Lord's Day services. "I tell him to get up, but he just rolls over and goes back to sleep. Hey, I don't want to make him go to church if he doesn't want to!" This sounds extremely spiritual, but it's really a "four-ball cop out" on the part of the father. The child's falsely assumed *autonomy* becomes the excuse for Dad's cowardly passivity.

An eleven-year-old player once obnoxiously defied my assistant basketball coach. When confronted with his sin, the boy refused to apologize by crossing his arms and putting on a stone face. At the end of the practice, the father appeared, and when informed of the controversy, he said, "You wouldn't want me to *make him* apologize, would you?" This had a noble sound to it, but was not wise. I believe the father should have taken the situation in hand by compelling his son to forgiveness upon threat of severe discipline. Instead, the boy whistled away.

Parenting calls upon us to *subdue* and *rule* the sinful hearts of our children. They are solemnly obligated to submit their minds and wills to father and mother. *Passive-purple-four-ballism* is not an option.

A wise father will *compel* his lazy teenager to ask his mother's forgiveness for not waking up Sunday morning when she told him to, will ensure that he gets to church, and will make certain that he's singing the hymns! After all, everything that has breath is obligated to praise the Lord (Psalm 150:6).

Remember, the commandment reads:

> **Exodus 20:12** *"Honor your father and your mother, that your days may be prolonged in the land which the LORD your God gives you."*

R. L. Dabney wisely discusses the authority that parents, under God, wield over the souls of their children:

> There is no power allowed to any creature under heaven over another responsible creature so wide as this providential power of the parent. Men speak of the Czar as the "Autocrat of Russians." They describe with a shudder that imperial power over the property, the liberty, and the life of the subject, unrestrained by constitution, law, jury, or appeal. But the power of a Czar over a subject is trifling compared with this parental power over children. . . .
>
> The parent has power almost to invade this sacred liberty of (the child's) soul. It is made both his privilege and his duty to impose the principles and the creed which he has sincerely adopted as the truth for himself upon the spirit of the child. Some men, it is known, vainly prate of the supposed obligation to leave the minds of their children independent and "unbiased" until they are mature enough to choose for themselves. But a moment's thought shows this unlawful and impossible. . . . One thing is certain, this young and plastic soul will take impress from somewhere — if not from the appointed and heaven-ordained hand of his parent, then from some other irresponsible hand, of man or evil angel. One might as well speak of immersing an open vessel in the ocean and having it remain empty as of having a youthful soul to grow up in society "unbiased," until it is qualified to elect its own creed most wisely.[2]

Fathers, we've been solemnly commissioned to "train up a child in the way he should go" (Proverbs 22:6a). Which way is this? This way is "in the discipline and instruction of the Lord." This way will require us to exercise assertive dominion. The Lord's recipe for a harvest of righteousness involves an aggressive planting, cultivating, and watering the hearts of our dear children.

Don't be a *passive-purple-four-ball* father.

25 / CHILD REARING: OUR SACRED COMMISSION

1 Robert Lewis Dabney, *Discussions of Robert Lewis Dabney* (Edinburgh: Banner of Truth, 1991), p.679

2 Ibid., pp.683-685

Chapter 26
Our Sinful Children

Who are these adorable little bundles of cuteness that we wrap up in towels after their baths, and with whom we delightfully roll around with on the carpet after dinner? Who are they that ask the most endearing of questions while we're tucking them into their beds after a long day? These are our children. But who are they really? What fundamentally are they made of? What's their nature?

A few months ago, our local newspaper reported a tragic story about a family who had raised a raccoon as a house pet. They treated it as a beagle; as a sweet, well tempered canine. But one afternoon, the mother went out into the yard to work, leaving her infant daughter in her crib, while the raccoon wandered the house. The result was a once beautiful little girl with a permanently disfigured face! This tragedy occurred because the parents foolishly failed to understand the *identity* and *nature* of the raccoon. It was not a domesticated house pet. It was a wild animal. Likewise, if parents are to properly raise their children under God, they've got to understand the *identity* and *nature* of their little ones. A misunderstanding here will bring tragic results.

So, who fundamentally, are our children?

1. According to the World

The secular psychologists and educators are very optimistic here. Their propaganda paints for us a very nice portrait of our offspring.

Some tell us that they're innocent darlings, born *morally neutral*, like a blank tablet just waiting to be written upon by their environment and experiences. This is the old *Behaviorism* of B. F. Skinner who taught that character outcome is determined exclusively by external influences. This view depicts our newborn children as those floating, cottonwood puffball seeds we see drifting about in the spring air.

They're suspended and weightless, pushed about by whatever puff of wind might pass by. So our morally neutral children are vulnerably pushed about by the influences of their parents and their environment. It's the blowing of these external influences, for evil or for good that exclusively determine the direction of a child's life.

More prevalent today are those who tell us that our children are born *basically good*. These authors, therapists, and educators assure us that the fundamental nature of our race is noble and virtuous. If we would just leave our children to themselves, without authoritatively intruding into their developing personalities, they'd grow up to be happy, loving, and fulfilled people. The *Human Potential Psychology* of Carl Rogers popularized this optimistic evaluation. This view depicts our newborns as helium-filled balloons. Leave them to themselves, and they'll ascend to noble heights of character. Firm parental interference and intervention will actually hinder the self-actualizing ascent of our children!

2. According to the Bible

The Scriptures give us an altogether different picture. Sure, at creation Adam was good, even very good (Genesis 1:31). But then came the serpent, the rebellion, the fall, the curse, and the expulsion from the garden. Good Adam and Eve became evil. Since then, with the single exception of the Bethlehem Babe, only *evil children* have been conceived and born.

> **Psalm 51:5** *Behold, I was brought forth in iniquity, And in sin my mother conceived me.*

> **Romans 5:19** *For as through the one man's disobedience the many were made sinners, even so through the obedience of the One the many will be made righteous.*

> **Romans 3:10ff** *as it is written, "There is none righteous, not even one; 11 There is none who understands, there is none who seeks for God; . . . 15 "<u>their feet are swift to shed blood</u>, . . . 18 "there is no fear of god before their eyes."*

Yes, this is the Lord's sobering diagnosis of even the most seemingly angelic of our newborns. They're rebels against God like their father

Adam; their direction is a rushing toward evil. Now, this doesn't mean that they're as bad as they could be. Certainly, we can see admirable qualities, such as that rare toddler who delights in sharing his toys. But in their hearts, they're fundamentally inclined against God.

> **Genesis 8:21a** *And the LORD smelled the soothing aroma; and the LORD said to Himself, "I will never again curse the ground on account of man, for the intent of man's heart is evil from his youth;*

> **Psalm 58:3** *The wicked are estranged from the womb; These who speak lies go astray from birth.*

So our children are not at all like floating cottonwood, puffball seeds, that is, morally neutral. Nor are they like rising helium balloons, basically good. To the contrary, the Bible depicts them like *descending bowling balls*, plummeting morally downward with a strong inclination and bent toward evil. And if their course is not arrested by aggressive intervention, they'll split hell wide open.

Who, fundamentally, are our children? They're *born rebels.*

3. According to Observation

The Bible unapologetically identifies our children as sinful rebels against God. They spurn His law, most flagrantly, the fifth commandment: "Honor your father and mother." It's hardly necessary to provide any supporting evidence.

If parents *passively* sit back and let their children *have their own way*, they won't *ascend* to be noble; they'll *descend* to be very evil. Just take a look at the present crop of twenty-first-century American youth and behold the spoiled harvest of permissive parenting.

> **Proverbs 29:15** *The rod and reproof give wisdom, But a child who gets his own way (KJV: left to himself) brings shame to his mother.*

Our children are born as sinful rebels against God. They natively spurn good. When left to themselves, they accelerate downward toward increasing evil. If their self-destructive course is to be arrested, they need aggressive intervention. We parents must courageously rise to the occasion by assertively exercising *manly dominion* over our children by seeking to *subdue* and *rule* in their lives. In many ways, their eternal destinies depend on it.

A passive-purple-four-ball approach would make us spectators to their spiritual suicides.

Chapter 27
Our Essential Confrontation

The two-year-old boy walks into his grandma's living room and sees a beautiful flower arrangement in the middle of the coffee table. Instinctively, he wants to touch it, and maybe even maul it. But his mother, sitting on the sofa says, "Joey, don't touch the flowers. No!" Joey fully understands, but is not in the mood to obey. He defiantly reaches for the flowers.

Now what's a mother to do? She could *remove* the flower arrangement and place it high atop the bookcase. She could remove her hairbrush from her purse and use this intriguing article to *divert* Joey's attention. Or she could physically *restrain* Joey by holding him straightjacket style in her lap. However, I believe that none of the above measures would be a biblical solution. Neither *confiscation*, *diversion*, nor *incarceration* would be appropriate. The child needs *confrontation*.

Simply put, we need to reject worldly techniques:

> **Exodus 20:12** *"Honor your father and your mother, that your days may be prolonged in the land which the LORD your God gives you..."*

> **Ephesians 6:1** *Children, obey your parents in the Lord, for this is right.*

In Joey's meeting the authority of his mother regarding the dried flowers, he's meeting the authority of his God and Maker, Who commands him to submissively obey and honor his parents. This is a solemn moment. It's no time for playing games. It's time for Joey to bend his will and submit to God. It's time for holy *confrontation*. Joey's will must be directly confronted. He needs to be required to obey.

Now, I realize that the typical secular psychologist is horrified by my analysis that calls for confrontation. But that is no surprise, because he knows neither the *identity* of Joey, nor the *expectation* God has placed on Joey. To the psychologist, Joey is basically good, and views principles like *honoring*, *obeying*, and *submitting* as developmentally stifling. Therefore, the psychologist recommends that we avoid at all cost the technique of confrontation. Keep the waters calm and don't capsize the little boy's boat!

Later that day, Joey may be riding in the grocery cart in the check-out aisle. He wants the colorful flashlight. Mom says, "No!" Joey throws a tantrum. Mom is embarrassed, so she tries to divert his attention with bribery. "Here, let's buy this box of mint candies. See the noise it makes when you shake it!" Or maybe: "When we get home, I'll give you some ice cream, if you'll please just be nice."

Maybe when he's older, Joey's told by his father that it's bedtime. Joey announces that he doesn't want to go to bed right now. Dad, wanting to avoid a collision with Joey's will, semi-apologetically gives an explanation for his command. "Now Joey, you know that if you don't go to bed right now, you'll be ornery tomorrow. It'll be best for us all in the long run if you'll just cooperate. Please!" Joey stomps angrily. Dad responds: "Hey, if you'll go up right now, I'll read you a book. What do you say, buddy?"

All of these non-confrontational strategies do great harm to the child. They evade and skirt the heart issue of a child's solemn need to submit his will to the authority of his parents (fifth commandment). They cower before the child with a dread to cross or challenge his will. When confrontation is avoided, and diversionary tactics are employed, the crucial issue of authority is left unaddressed. Willful submission under God is never rendered. The sad harvest is an unmanageable, undisciplined, ungodly young adult. Today, we're seeing a bumper crop of them.

Employ Biblical Measures

Biblical psychology insists we must confront the wills of our children. And the Scriptures tell us precisely how.

> **Proverbs 29:15** *The rod and reproof give wisdom, But a child who gets his own way brings shame to his mother.*

Proverbs 20:30 *Stripes that wound scour away evil, And strokes reach the innermost parts.*

When a child premeditatedly challenges and defies a parent's authority, by purposefully crossing a verbally drawn line, he must be given reason to regret it. The *rod* (Hebrew: *shebet:* stick, branch, *paddle*) is an eloquent communicator. The Lord tells us it's able to register a wholesome impression on young minds, as *strokes reach the inmost parts*. It penetrates far deeper into a little soul than logical argumentation. It teaches its student to *honor* (weigh as heavy verses blow off as light) father and mother. The rod confronts a child's rebellious will like no other device.

Proverbs 22:15 *Foolishness is bound up in the heart of a child; The rod of discipline will remove it far from him.*

Whenever a child's behavior represents a defiant challenge of parental authority, it's not time for "a time out." The devil within the child's heart is rearing his rebellious head. It's no time to lie back until the serpent retreats back underground. It's time to give a strong blow to that serpentine head by a principled spanking to the child's behind.

We wonder why Joey keeps on disobeying, while we keep on letting him rule the field. Parents must exercise *manly dominion* by committing themselves to subdue and rule in the field of their offspring. And this project is not one for the faint of heart.

John S. C. Abbott's insightful book, *The Mother At Home,* written in 1833, is filled with good, old fashioned, biblical counsel, untainted by the nonsense of modern "politically correct" psychology. The following is an actual contest of wills described by John Abbot's pen. Note the name of the little boy in the account:

> A gentleman, sitting by his fireside one evening, with his family around him, took the spelling-book and called upon one of his little sons to come and read. *John* was about four years old. He knew all the letters of the alphabet perfectly, but happened at that moment to be in rather a sullen humor, and was not at all disposed to gratify his father. Very reluctantly he came as he was bid, but when his father pointed with his knife to the first letter of the alphabet, and said, "What letter is that, John?" he could get no answer. John looked upon the book, sulky and silent.

"My son," said the father, pleasantly, "you know the letter A."

"I cannot say A," said John.

"You must," said the father, in a serious and decided tone. "What letter is that?"

John refused to answer.

The contest was now fairly commenced. John was willful, and determined that he could not read. His father knew that it would be ruinous to his son to allow him to conquer. He felt that he must, at all hazards subdue him. He took him into another room, and punished him. He then returned, and again showed John the letter. But John still refused to name it. The father again retired with his son, and punished him more severely. But it was unavailing; the stubborn child still refused to name the letter, and when the father inflicted punishment as he dared to do it, and still the child, with his whole frame in agitation, refused to yield.

The father was suffering from the most intense solicitude. He regretted exceedingly that he had been drawn into the contest. He had already punished his child with a severity which he feared to exceed. And yet the willful sufferer stood before him, sobbing and trembling, but apparently as unyielding as a rock.

I have often heard that parent mention the acuteness of his feelings at that moment. His heart was bleeding at the pain which he had been compelled to inflict upon his son. He knew that the question was now to be settled, who should be master. And after his son had withstood so long and so much, he greatly feared the result.

The mother sat by, suffering, of course, most acutely, but perfectly satisfied that it was their duty to subdue the child, and that in such a trying hour a mother's feelings must not interfere.

With a heavy heart the father again took the hand of his son to lead him out of the room for further punishment. But, to his inconceivable joy, the child shrunk from enduring any more suffering, and cried, "Father, I'll tell the letter." The father with feelings not easily conceived, took the book and pointed to the letter.

"A," said John, distinctly and fully.

"And what is that?" said the father, pointing to the next letter.

"B," said John.

"And what is that?"

"C," he continued.

"And what is that?" pointing again to the first letter.

"A," said the now humbled child.

"Now carry the book to your mother, and tell her what the letter is."

"What is that, my son?" said the mother.

"A," said John. He was evidently perfectly subdued. The rest of the children were sitting by, and they saw the contest, and they saw where the victory was. And John learnt a lesson which he never forgot, that his father had an arm too strong for him. He learnt that it was the safest and happiest course for him to obey. He learned never again to wage such an unequal warfare.

But perhaps some one says it was cruel to punish the child so severely. Cruel! It was mercy and love. It would indeed have been cruel had the father, in that hour, been unfaithful, and shrunk from his painful duty. The passions he was then, with so much self-sacrifice, striving to subdue, if left unchecked, would in all probability have been a curse to his friends. It is by no means improbable that upon the decisions of that hour depended the character and happiness of that child for life, and even for eternity. It is far from improbable that, had he then conquered, all future efforts to subdue him would have been in vain, and that he would have broken away from all restraint, and have been miserable in life, and lost in death. Cruelty! The Lord preserve children from the tender mercies of those who so regret self-denying kindness.[1]

Proverbs 13:24 *He who spares his rod hates his son, But he who loves him disciplines him diligently.*

We must not hate our children by passively, naively, and cowardly curling up into *passive-purple four-balls.* We must courageously stand up like men to subdue their young hearts for their good and God's glory.

Employ manly dominion by faithfully *confronting* your children.

1 John S. C. Abbot, *The Mother at Home* (Sterling, VA: Grace Abounding Ministries, 1984), pp.29-31

Chapter 28
Our Saving Culmination

Our goal in child rearing is not simply to train our children to be good spellers, to avoid unnecessary breath mint purchases at grocery check-out lanes, to preserve our mothers-in-laws' coffee table flower arrangements, or even to enjoy tranquil home lives. Our ultimate goal is the sweet submission of their hearts and the eternal salvation of their souls. Our hope is to subdue their souls for Christ.

The disciplinary intervention of spanking isn't like the shocking of a laboratory rat by simply giving negative stimuli for undesirable behavior. I was once standing in a church lobby having a discussion with a mother of many. One of her children ran by shouting loudly. The mother, showing great athletic agility, spun around, and while her son was in mid-stride, swatted him firmly across his fanny, and told him to stop running and be quiet. The little guy continued on running and shouting. She then looked up to me, and shrugging her shoulders said, "See, spanking doesn't work with him!"

A Spanking Formula

In my mind, the biblical use of the rod (spanking) requires a number of basic features:

1. *The Finding of a Private Place*—In your home, it may be a bedroom, bathroom, or walk-in closet. There, you can gain your child's full attention, away from distractions and peers. In the last chapter's "Letter A" account, the father retired to another room.

> **Proverbs 5:1a** *My son, give attention to my wisdom…*

2. *The Speaking of Necessary Reproof*—Clear verbal instruction must be communicated to the offending child. "You're being spanked because you're stubbornly refusing to recite the letter A. You're disobeying me and God, who tells you to honor me in His fifth commandment."

> **Proverbs 29:15a** *The rod <u>and reproof</u> give wisdom...*

3. *The Securing of a Submissive Posture*—Outward posture is important. A little child who is permitted to kick, twist, and fight off his spanking is hardly honoring his parent! But be realistic and don't expect perfection.

> **Lamentations 3:30** *Let him give his cheek to the smiter; Let him be filled with reproach.*

4. *The Delivering of Sufficient Blows*—Parents should target the well-padded buttocks above the thighs. Thick diapers or jeans as a barrier between will probably not produce the therapeutic pain and sorrow necessary for improvement. A painless spanking will produce bitter cynicism instead of sweet submission. "Spank him till he's sweet," was the advice of a wise mother to her spanking husband.

> **Hebrews 12:11** *All discipline for the moment seems not to be joyful, but <u>sorrowful</u>; yet to those who have been trained by it, afterwards it yields the peaceful fruit of righteousness.*

5. *The Reconciling of the Sinner*—After the spanking, the child is required to apologize for his sin and request forgiveness. "Dad, I'm sorry for refusing to say the letter A. Please forgive me." He may then spontaneously bury himself in the warm reconciling embrace of his father, who instructs him to prayerfully confess his sin to God and ask forgiveness.

> **1 John 1:9** *If we confess our sins, He is faithful and righteous to forgive us our sins and to cleanse us from all unrighteousness.*

6. *The Reenacting of the Situation*—Little John returns back to the scene of the crime and is told to recite aloud the letters A through C.

Ephesians 6:1 *Children, obey your parents in the Lord, for this is right.*

An Evangelistic Tool

Many parents have found that the principled use of the rod functions as an amazingly effective tool for evangelism. Figuratively speaking, the Lord uses the rod as a blessed scalpel that cuts through calloused layers of sin, and exposes tender issues of the heart.

One evening many years ago, I was forced to discipline one of my sons for an offense for which he'd been repeatedly spanked in the past. As my little boy stood tearfully with his hands on the bed waiting for the "sufficient blows," he turned to me utterly perplexed with himself and loudly blurted out, "Dad, why don't I obey?"

Ah, look how open and laid bare his rebellious heart is now to his own eyes! The cute and crafty camouflage has been removed. He finally sees his despicable rebellion for what it is! At a moment like this, he's not far from the kingdom. In his words, I heard a faint echo of the Apostle Paul's frustrated laments:

> **Romans 7:13** *Therefore did that which is good become a cause of death for me? May it never be! Rather it was sin, in order that it might be shown to be sin by effecting my death through that which is good, that through the commandment <u>sin might become utterly sinful</u>.*

> **Romans 7:24** *<u>Wretched man that I am</u>! Who will set me free from the body of this death?*

What a blessed time I had holding this little plowed up soul while his shoulders tearfully heaved in my arms. I told him why he keeps on disobeying. "Son, you have a sinful and very bad heart. You need the Lord Jesus to forgive you of your sin and give you a new heart. You need to pray to Him right now, and ask that He'd have mercy on your soul so that you don't go to hell, but to heaven"

The confronting rod thus becomes a tutor to Christ!

Our children desperately need us to arouse ourselves with principles of manly dominion. They need us to early and courageously seek to subdue their sinful passions. Not only does this aggressive intervention lay the groundwork for such character virtues as self-control, self-denial, submission to authority, etc., but it also plows up their hearts, softening them for the seeds of the gospel.

In this great mission of child rearing, may the Lord keep us from passively hiding behind our newspapers, computer screens, wives' skirts, and our aversions to conflict. God help us from curling up into passive-purple four-balls. God help us to aggressively charge out onto the battlefield and fight for the souls of our children.

Manly Dominion in Romance Managing

A few years ago, I was provoked by an automobile advertisement in a national news magazine. On the upper portion of the page was a hand written postcard addressed to:

Mom & Dad
544 Washington Rd.
Grosse Point, MI 48230

It read:

Dear Mom & Dad,

L.A. is awesome!!!
I met a guy!! He plays bass in a band!
We stayed up all night on the beach and watched the sun rise!
Then we rode to Venice on his motorcycle!
Can't wait for you to meet him!!!

Love, Julie :) XOX

Then on the lower portion of the page, it read:

Haven't you got enough to worry about? We can't take away all the headaches your kids give you. But we can prescribe the Chevy Lumina. Solid. Reliable.

What kind of a father passively sits back as a helpless bystander while his daughter leaps recklessly into potentially dangerous romantic situations? The assumption of the advertisement is that today's parents can only ring their hands and hope for the best! And you know what? That's just the passive-purple-four-ball approach that dominates in America today, even in professing Christian homes!

Twenty-first century parents have been duped into thinking that all they can do is sit back and hear postcard reports of their children's inevitable romantic exploits.

A man with a biblical dominion mindset won't allow himself to sit back as a passive observer. He'll not leave his offspring to themselves, to navigate the dangerous minefield of romance on their own. He'll get up off his sofa. He'll assertively strive to provide guidance and wisdom for his child's relationships with members of the opposite gender. Such relationships lead to the making of life's second most important decision: "Who will be my spouse?" Parents, and especially fathers, are commissioned by God to be heavily involved participants, not aloof, handcuffed bystanders. We're obligated to step up and engage ourselves in wise and tactful *romance managing*.

Chapter 29
Manly Dominion in Romance Managing: Fatherly Giving in Marriage

Back in the winter of 1982, I took a deep breath and said, “Mr. Becker, could I talk with you, all alone?” He suggested that the basement would give us the best privacy, and before I knew it, I was staring eye to eye with my darling Dianne’s father. With his intimidating German brogue, he asked me, “So Mark, what’s on your mind?”

“Mr. Becker, I love your daughter, and am asking if you’ll give me her hand in marriage?”

Now, why did I do that? Was this request of mine merely a sentimental option, or was it a biblical obligation? After all, Dianne was twenty-three years old. She’d been able to vote for nearly five years. What authority did this gray-haired man wield over her marital plans?

My family was recently watching a video movie called, *The Father of the Bride*. The groom-to-be (whom the bride’s parents had met only minutes before) sat alongside his fiancée and announced to her parents that they were engaged, and would be married in January. The father’s mouth dropped open in disbelief. But, of course, he was depicted as a naïve dinosaur whose fatherly instincts of paternal authority was hopelessly outdated and needed to get up to speed with the twenty-first century. Right there, I stopped the tape, and inserted some brief comments on the Bible’s teaching on the father’s role in *giving in marriage*.

Yes, God commissions fathers with the solemn task of *romance managing*.

> **Exodus 22:16-17** *"And if a man seduces a virgin who is not engaged, and lies with her, he must pay a dowry for her to be his wife. 17 If her father absolutely refuses to give her to him, he shall pay money equal to the dowry for virgins...*

Here's a less than ideal scenario. Maybe a shepherdess in a hidden valley is spied by a farmer boy who entices her into sexual union. Her virginity is lost. The two agree to marry. The farmer boy informs the father of their plans, implying it's a done deal. Not so, say the Scriptures. It's the father's decision that rules. The daughter is the father's to give or withhold. The ultimate right of approval or refusal belongs to Dad.

The text is very clear. The father of the daughter—not the daughter, not the seducer, not true love, not Hollywood—decides. Mundane old Dad makes the decision. Now obviously the daughter had seen something in this young man. But the father may not have seen it, or perhaps he did see it, but had a different opinion of it.[1]

As old fashioned as it might seem, the Bible teaches that Fathers have an important jurisdiction over whom their children marry, their daughters in particular.

> **Deuteronomy 7:1-3** *"When the LORD your God shall bring you into the land where you are entering to possess it, and shall clear away many nations before you, the Hittites and the Girgashites and the Amorites and the Canaanites and the Perizzites and the Hivites and the Jebusites, seven nations greater and stronger than you, 2 and when the LORD your God shall deliver them before you, and you shall defeat them, then you shall utterly destroy them. You shall make no covenant with them and show no favor to them. 3 "Furthermore, you shall not intermarry with them; you shall not give your daughters to their sons, nor shall you take their daughters for your sons.*

This *fatherly giving* of their daughters in marriage, and *taking of daughters-in-law*, is acknowledged by the covenant renewal pledge during the days of Nehemiah.

> **Nehemiah 10:29-30** *are joining with their kinsmen, their nobles, and are taking on themselves a curse and an oath to walk in God's law, which was given through Moses, God's servant, and to keep and to observe all the*

> *commandments of GOD our Lord, and His ordinances and His statutes; 30 and that we will not give our daughters to the peoples of the land or take their daughters for our sons...*

It may be objected that this fatherly jurisdiction is merely a part of *temporary* ceremonial or civil law, no longer relevant for the new covenant Christian. But the New Testament, and the Lord Jesus Himself invalidate this objection. *Giving in marriage* did not begin at Sinai. It's as old as creation itself, when the Lord *gave* his daughter Eve to Adam as his bride.

> **Matthew 24:38** *For as in those days which were before the flood they were eating and drinking, they were marrying and giving in marriage, until the day that Noah entered the ark...*

Fatherly *giving in marriage* held sway from creation to Noah, and should be practiced on earth until the Lord's return and the final resurrection of the dead.

> **Matthew 22:29-30** *But Jesus answered and said to them, "You are mistaken, not understanding the Scriptures, or the power of God. 30 "For in the resurrection they neither marry, nor are given in marriage, but are like angels in heaven..."*

The Apostle Paul *assumes the enduring, solemn obligation of fatherly giving in marriage* as he instructs Corinthian fathers regarding their duty toward their virgin daughters.

> **1 Corinthians 7:36-38** *But if any man thinks that he is acting unbecomingly toward his virgin daughter, if she should be of full age, and if it must be so, let him do what he wishes, he does not sin; let her marry. 37 But he who stands firm in his heart, being under no constraint, but has authority over his own will, and has decided this in his own heart, to keep his own virgin daughter, he will do well. 38 So then both he who gives his own virgin daughter in marriage does well, and he who does not give her in marriage will do better.*

It is, therefore, undeniably true that the Bible teaches that the authority of a father clearly extends to his children's romantic interests, particularly his daughter's, whom he must *give*, if she is to marry. This solemn commission can't be dismissed by an extreme horror story of a cruel father keeping his daughter locked up in spinsterhood. Fathers are also obligated to act becomingly toward their virgin daughters (1 Corinthians 7:26). Dad must be reasonable in evaluating a suitor. He must not unreasonably withhold marriage beyond the flower of her youth, etc. In some situations, a Christian child may possibly have the right and prerogative to marry in spite of contrary parental direction. The daughter would be wise to seek pastoral counsel in such circumstances. These qualifications that call a father to *act* becomingly, are important ones. But the bottom line of fatherly authority is clear.

Back in 1982, when I asked that stately gray-haired man for his daughter's hand in marriage, I wasn't merely following a sentimental tradition; I was submitting to a biblical obligation.

Fathers, we've been commissioned by God to get deeply involved in our children's romantic lives. We must think and act biblically. It's no wonder that daughters write postcards from L.A. informing parents of co-ed nights on the beach, and that their suitors appear and *inform* fathers of scheduled wedding dates. Modern Dads have *passively* disrespected their fatherhood by abdicating their *protector role*. The disrespect of their children is a mere echo of the disrespect fathers have of their own office.

We must think and act biblically. A father's monitoring his children's romantic relationships and determining for himself the godliness, intelligence, maturity, and diligence of a daughter's suitor is not obnoxious *intruding*. It's biblical fathering.

The wisdom of God's commission for parental romance management is clear.

1. Youth is a vulnerable season.

The importance of the choice of one's physical spouse can't be overstated. A life of joy or sorrow hangs in the balance. And the Lord hasn't left teens and twenties to make that decision alone. He's built into their lives a competent *guidance system* in the presence of their parents. Young people, who've barely been around the block, are ill-equipped to assess character, foresee danger, and choose a partner on their own.

Proverbs 7:6-7 *For at the window of my house I looked out through my lattice, 7 And I saw among the naive, I discerned among the youths, A young man lacking sense...*

2. Romance is potentially dangerous.

In Walt Disney's *Bambi*, the rabbit Thumper is disgusted with the effect the pretty doe has on the young buck Bambi. Bambi has become *twitterpated*, which means he's head-over-heels lost his common sense. The romantically involved young person typically enters into an emotional fog of *twitterpation* and doesn't see very clearly.

Proverbs 31:30a *Charm is deceitful and beauty is vain...*

She's so beautiful, sweet, and delightful. He's so handsome, polite, and strong. Love will get us through. Let's not get bogged down with such mundane things as spiritual credibility, doctrinal compatibility, and financial solvency.

Modern conventional wisdom says: "Well, they're in love, and there's really nothing that parents can do about it." Being "in love" has become an undisputed authority, a gripping nebulous force with which we're told, we can't argue.

3. Young women are easily preyed upon.

A father has been commissioned to protect his daughter from the sheer strength of male suitors. The testosterone-filled male gender is natively more forceful and powerful than the female. Peter calls wives the "weaker vessel" (1 Peter 3: 7). Men typically have the capacity to physically, emotionally, and relationally *manhandle* young women with their aggressiveness. What a blessed safeguard it is for a young woman, already enamored with the prospects of a white dress, a wedding march, a rice shower, and a honeymoon, to have to say to a persuasive suitor: "Well, you'll have to talk to my father about that."

Oh, I know that Hollywood fights hard against parental participation by producing Romeo and Juliet plots that cast loving parents as obstructionist villains standing in the way of "true love." But by God's grace, Christians must nurture in their families a biblical counter culture, built on the cornerstone: "Honor your father and mother." Young people ought to become convinced: "I'm not an independent free agent.

I'm solemnly accountable to my parents regarding whom I marry." Such a framework, humbly applied and Spiritually aided, can avoid the all too common marital disasters of our day.

But the blessed dividends of parental romance managing won't be enjoyed as long as fathers, with *purple-four-ball passivity*, allow themselves to conform to the "spectator" pattern of the world. We fathers must act like men. We've got to offset the cultural onslaught by teaching our children early on the biblical perspective. If we were watching a video where *Bambi* and his "twitterpation," or *The Father of the Bride* and his lack of counsel are displayed, we'd do well to *stop the tape* and insert words in season. We need to, so help us God, grow in them such a holy trust, confidence, and love toward us, that they wouldn't even think about getting married without Dad's (and Mom's) approval.

John Angell James wisely advised young people to faithfully confide in their God-ordained counselors:

> When the subject (of a romantic interest) comes fairly before your attention, *make it known immediately to your parents.* Conceal nothing from them. Abhor the very idea of clandestine connections, as a violation of every duty you owe to God and man. There is nothing heroic in secret correspondence. The silliest girls and the weakest men can maintain it, and have been most frequently engaged in it. Spurn the individual who would come between you and your natural guardians. Hearken to the opinion of your parents with all the deference that is due to it. Rare are the cases in which you should act in opposition to their wishes.[2]

Certainly, these perspectives reprove the hand-pocketing, shoulder-shrugging, lip-zipping father who passively watches his child wander unprotected into potentially dangerous romances.

29 / FATHERLY GIVING IN MARRIAGE

1 Douglas Wilson, *Her Hand in Marriage* (Moscow, ID: Canon Press, 1997), p.28
2 John Angell James, *The Christian Father's Present to His Children* (Morgan, PA: Soli Deo Gloria, 1993; originally printed in 1853), p.367

Chapter 30
Fatherly Evaluating in Dating

Young people who conform to the romance practices of their surrounding, corrupt culture can come to great harm.

> **Genesis 34:1-3** *Now Dinah the daughter of Leah, whom she had borne to Jacob, went out to visit the daughters of the land. 2 And when Shechem the son of Hamor the Hivite, the prince of the land, saw her, he took her and lay with her by force. 3 And he was deeply attracted to Dinah the daughter of Jacob, and he loved the girl and spoke tenderly to her.*

Where was Jacob while his daughter was being taken advantage of by this Canaanite playboy named Shechem? In Genesis 34, Jacob seems to be in a bit of a *spiritual backslide*. Instead of continuing on to Bethel, where he'd vowed to build an altar to God (28:19; 31:13), he stopped short near the trade crossroads of Shechem, where he purchased land and settled in to mingle with the Canaanite culture. This was a decision he lived to regret. In Genesis 35:1-4, we hear the Lord arousing Jacob out of his funk: "Arise, go to Bethel . . . and make an altar there . . . Put away the foreign gods which are among you . . . " I believe the "Dinah disaster" can at least partially be traced back to a father who was spiritually negligent in overseeing his daughter's social life.

Jacob acted like a *passive-purple four-ball*. Regarding Dinah's social habits, Daddy apparently said, "When in Canaan, do as the Canaanites." That's just what many Christian fathers are doing today regarding their children's romance habits. "When in America, do as the Americans." This is a decision many live to regret.

A godly *man of dominion* will refuse to *conform* to the patterns of the world. He'll rise up and carefully *evaluate* the Canaanite status quo, and boldly reject any elements that would endanger his children's well being. He'll biblically evaluate the contemporary *dating game* and determine for himself whether his son or daughter ought to play.

"But Dad, everybody's doing it," doesn't *rule* the day. It's Dad, and his, "As for me and my house . . ." that *subdues* the issue and *rules* the day.

Let's evaluate the contemporary dating game.

Here's a sketch of the romantic history of a typical (actually, quite conservative) young man growing up in today's culture. By age nine, he realizes it's popular to like a particular girl in his class or church. By age ten, he's already paired off behind a vacant barn with a girl to give her lip kisses and long embraces. By age twelve, he knows if you're not going with someone, you're not cool. By age thirteen, he overhears during the Christmas holidays his aunt asking his mother, "Doesn't he have a girlfriend yet?" By age fourteen, he's consistently phoning his girlfriend most nights. By age fifteen, the nightlife and parties give him ample opportunities to go far beyond kissing. By age sixteen, he's got a license to drive, opening up more opportunities for being alone with a girl at the coffee shop, the movies, a scenic overlook, or in her basement. With the car, he doesn't have to be home until well after midnight. By his college years, he's dated a whole buffet of girls, with whom rights to a physical relationship have been assumed.

At first glance, a parent may ask, "So what's wrong with that? That's the way I did it; and I survived!" A well-respected pastor once wrote: "People survive plane crashes too, some of them without a scratch, and we should be happy about it. But this acknowledgment does not disqualify us from opposing the general habit of plane crashes."

Furthermore, think back. Do you really want your children to experience everything ***you've*** experienced? Most of us believing parents, whose youth mirrored the above scenario, are ashamed of many of our actions, and can only marvel at God's grace that kept us from destroying our souls. In reality, we're just the *survivors*, and some very scarred survivors at that, while many of our peers passed through this cultural minefield and lost their souls. Surely, we seek better for our children than mere *scarred survival*.

We're naïve if we think this generation is playing the same tame version of the game we played. I've read that in many youth circles that what the passionate kiss goodnight was to the previous generation, impure intimacy is to this one.

1. Historical Perspective

The present dating game hasn't been around that long. Don't think it's always been this way. Prior to the 1900's, the phenomenon of single, young people pairing off and spending multiple hours together all alone was relatively unknown. *Calling* was much more common. A young man who was interested in a young lady would visit her home, usually under the watchful eye of her parents. The two young people might sit together on a porch or in a parlor, with fatherly oversight only a threshold away. Outside social activities were town celebrations and church events, typically chaperoned by parents or familiar adults. The watchful eyes of the community generally supervised relationships.

Dating, as we know it today, basically started with the urbanization of 1900 through 1920 helped by crowded apartments and tenements that had no private sitting room. Here, "going out" began, providing young couples a previously unknown independence. They could get lost in the crowd of the big city. The development of movie theatres and automobiles imparted "tickets to liberation" from chaperoned supervision. Increased participation in higher education (high school and college), fashioned a now segregated *youth culture*. Trendy magazines began to appeal to the new subculture. "Going steady" became a mark of popularity among teens.

The twentieth century produced a huge leap. Couples began the century chaperoned on the family front porch. They ended the century alone, late at night, in a private automobile. Fornication, use of contraceptives, illegitimate pregnancies, and abortions has become tragically common. Ill-advised marriages, easy divorces, and broken families have littered the landscape. Such is the spoiled harvest of the contemporary "dating game."

Fathers, are we wise to passively conform to the four-ball worldlings around us?

2. Emotional Perspective

Back in 1952, Dwight Harvey Small critiqued the emotionally immature relationships that often result from the "dating game" that is inherently void of depth and parental input:

> It must be noted that young people confront the need for making the distinction between romantic infatuation and love when they are emotionally least able to do so. The decision comes when they are caught up in a highly-charged emotional atmosphere, and are acting more on the basis of emotional compulsion than on rational judgment. . . .

> Romantic infatuation is the ground upon which is erected America's greatest cult, the cult of romance.... The entertainment and advertising worlds promote the great American worship of romance.... It makes up the colossal fairy story at the heart of our culture.
>
> The fairy story is usually told something like this: "I am a very attractive and lovable person, fascinating and desirable in every way. But I managed to go unnoticed for a long time. The reason for that was that the one and only person in this universe had not come my way. There was one just made for me and for no other, and at the right moment he was to come into my life. Then suddenly he appeared! In that moment our eyes met and I knew he was for me. He was my dream, my inspiration! He had everything! He was tall, tan, and terrific! We kissed and I knew I could not live without him. This was love, because I was tingling with excitement all over. Nothing mattered now except that we were together. How could anything else be important but this? We would live only for each other in perfect bliss....
>
> There could be no reason to wait a moment longer. With his scintillating sense of humor I knew we would never disagree about anything. Our love for each other would hurdle all obstacles as though they were nothing. Brought together by the hand of fate, we must *obey* and marry before it's too late! You dare not put off love for it might die if not acted on right now." And so they married and lived happily ever after in the delightful ecstasy of marital bliss![1]

But reality doesn't often match the fairy tale. Marriages built on the shifting sands of romantic infatuation don't last very long. Contrary to the modern trend, the Bible builds the marital relationship on the cornerstone of a covenantal commitment and act of the will.

> **Ephesians 5:25** *Husbands, love your wives, just as Christ also loved the church and gave Himself up for her...*

Choosing the love of one's life is a decision that ought to be based on rational analysis, not mere emotional romance. Lemuel's mother provides her son with a practical checklist of character traits that must be rationally considered.

Proverbs 31:10 *An excellent wife, who can find? For her worth is far above jewels. . . .*

Her checklist goes on to describe such practical attributes as diligence, responsibility, industriousness, selflessness, trustworthiness, financial savvy, prudence in speech, early-rising, strong maternal instincts, and foresight. Such things can be best observed and evaluated in practical, domestic settings.

But the contemporary dating game caters not to the rational, but to the emotional. It calculatedly whisks a couple off to a make-believe world (to a theatre, restaurant, or sports arena), detaching the couple from familial and practical life. There each can become a play actor where he or she can impersonate the ideal dating partner, and creatively register the desired romantic impression.

Fathers, do not conform to the world around you!

1 Dwight Harvey Small, *Design for Christian Marriage* (New York: Bantam Books, 1952), pp.130-131

Chapter 31
Fatherly Overseeing of Relationships

A number of years ago, I taught through this material at a men's conference in Florida. During the final session on *Romance Managing*, a single young woman who was helping the ladies prepare the men's dinner was attentively listening in an adjacent hallway. As I began to speak about the need for fathers to aggressively step up and protect their daughters from dating-game dangers, big tears welled up in her eyes. She confided in someone nearby that she yearned for her father to take a stand as her protector. She felt so vulnerable and so let down by her father whose passive negligence had contributed to the many scars she now bore.

What's a loving father to do? A number of good materials are available which in depth discuss wholesome principles for God-honoring courtship. Here, I'll just address the crucial need for a father to assertively oversee relationship pacing.

The contemporary dating game encourages participants to begin at a very young age. Romantic pairing off often begins before a child reaches his teen years! This is dangerous stuff. In Genesis 2, the Lord paired up the first couple, Adam and Eve, and left them to be alone together. This pairing up was clearly marriage focused. The relationship was soon consummated with physical intimacy, as "the two became one flesh" (2:24). This physical intimacy is the natural direction and destination of a male and female romantic relationship. Samson and Delilah weren't just playing monopoly; neither were Shechem and Dinah.

I know everyone's doing it, but why would a father permit his child to get on a train that leads to the land of sexual intimacy when he or she's got no business arriving there anytime soon? It's a formula for disaster. Do we want our children engaging in premarital sex, as are most contemporary dating participants? Then, until they're reasonably close to being ready for marriage, they shouldn't be boarding the romance train. Marital ripeness and eligibility entails multiple factors including spiritual maturity, emotional seasoning, educational advancement, vocational readiness, and financial capability. For most, ripeness in these important areas won't be reached until their early twenties.

> Be guided in this affair by the dictates of prudence. Never think of forming a connection till there is a rational prospect of temporal provision. I am not quite sure that the present age is in this respect more prudent than the past. It is all very pretty and pleasing for two young people to sing of love in a cottage, and draw picturesque views of two affectionate hearts struggling together amidst the difficulties of life; but these pictures are seldom realized. Connections that begin in imprudence generally end in wretchedness. Young people who marry without the consent of their parents, when that consent is withheld, not from caprice, but discretion, often find that they are not united like two doves, by a silken thread, but like two of Samson's foxes, with a firebrand between them. I call it little else than wickedness to marry without the rational prospect of temporal support.[1]

> **Proverbs 24:27** *Prepare your work outside, And make it ready for yourself in the field; Afterwards, then, build your house.*

> The house building probably means the founding of a family (14:1): a matter that must wait its turn till *afterwards*. As, in a rural economy, well-worked fields justify and nourish the farmhouse, so a well-ordered life (in things material and immaterial) should be established before marriage.[2]

A biblical parent, the father in particular, will view himself as the conductor and engineer of his child's romance railroad. If his son will not be eligible to prudently marry until he has finished his accounting degree at age twenty-one or twenty-two, he'll strongly recommend that his son not even get on the romance train until he's eighteen or nineteen. In fact, if the son is living under the father's roof, "recommend" is probably too weak a word. Even when he's welcomed aboard the train, the pace of any relationship will need to be wisely monitored. If a six-hundred mile train ride needs to last three days, you better not be traveling sixty mph after a couple of hours, especially since slowing down is a very difficult maneuver. Once per month social contacts would be very suitable in the early going.

> **Ecclesiastes 3:1ff** *There is an appointed time for everything. And there is a time for every event under heaven . . . 5b A time to embrace, and a time to shun embracing.*

A biblical father will be diligently aggressive in assessing and in teaching his children what time it is.

Sons vs. Daughters

It's important to note that daughters and not sons are biblically "given in marriage." At the wedding, the question is rightly asked, "Who gives this woman to this man?" The correct answer is rightly to come from the father, "I do!" In any romance, it's the father of the maiden who holds the ultimate authority in governing the relationship.

With our sons, once we've deemed them old enough to enter into a relationship with a maiden, our fatherly management should come to them in the form of earnest advice and strong counsel. Hopefully by now, we have their hearts, and they take our words as heavy. This is especially important because oftentimes the maiden's father is an untaught and passive man who's willing to conform to the *dating game*. In such circumstances, a wise young man will conscientiously seek out and concur with his parents' guidance. But parents should discreetly keep in mind their sons' manhood. Don't exasperate them.

Doug Wilson writes in *Future Men*:

> Fathers who want to control the details of their sons, marrying are, ironically, behaving in a way that will make a very poor husband out of any son who puts up with it. When a man marries, he is stepping into headship and responsibility. He cannot do this well if he has never done it before. If right up to the wedding his mother is cutting his meat for him, and his father is tying his shoes, don't look for *that* marriage to wind up in the hall of fame.[3]

But surely a son's manhood doesn't absolve him of his solemn obligation to honor his parents by weighing heavily their wise counsel. The Proverbial Father continues with "My Son...My Son...My Son..." counsel deep into his boy's manhood. His student is old enough, and mature enough, to heed words like these:

> **Proverbs 5:18-19** *Let your fountain be blessed and rejoice in the wife of your youth. As a loving doe, let her breasts satisfy you at all times; Be exhilarated always with her love.*

If a college-age son thinks he's matured beyond the stage of needing his father's earnest counsel, he's dead wrong. The Word of God calls him to a pliable humility.

> **1 Peter 5:5** *You younger men, likewise, be subject to your elders; and all of you, clothe yourselves with humility toward one another, for GOD IS OPPOSED TO THE PROUD, BUT GIVES GRACE TO THE HUMBLE.*

The full-grown son is also solemnly obligated to bend his ear to his mother's marital advice:

> **Proverbs 31:1ff** *The words of King Lemuel, the oracle which his mother taught him. 2 What O my son? And what, O son of my womb? And what, O son of my vows? 3 Do not give your strength to women, Or your ways to that which destroys kings...10 An excellent wife, who can find? For her worth is far above jewels...30 Charm is deceitful and beauty is vain, But a women who fears the LORD, she shall be praised.*

It must be admitted that this entire chapter is built on the optimistic hope that our grown children will be made tender hearted and wisely submissive by the Spirit's power. A proud and unruly son or daughter can axe this framework to splinters. Furthermore, an out of town college and dormitory situation may really complicate things. Lest the Lord builds a house, parents labor in vain! I know it's challenging, young men; but maintain and stay the God-honoring course. You won't regret it.

Daughters, on the other hand, should be more thoroughly supervised (cf. 1 Corinthians 7:36-38). The father is responsible to more specifically set her relationship ground rules. If a suitor wants to initiate a relationship with my daughter, he'll need to get her father's approval. Note that her father's questioning, investigating, and background checking will not be rude intruding, but faithful fathering. If the suitor wants to visit my daughter, email her, telephone her, spend time with her; or accompany her to a special event, he'll need to first gain *my* approval. I am her guardian and protector.

Now understand that this relationship management project doesn't begin when she turns eighteen or nineteen. If it's going to practically work, I've got to have her heart! It's not just a matter of a father putting his foot down (though at times such foot planting is essential). It's a matter of starting early, when she's still little; of acting like a man while she is growing up. The girl who sees her selfish father habitually refusing to take her sliding or swimming because he was unwilling to miss his TV sports, may have trouble being convinced that he ultimately has her prosperity in mind. A father who's been selfish, overbearing, and lazy for nearly two decades ought not be surprised that he doesn't have his daughter's heart. Oh, she's obligated to submit to him, but it won't be easy for her.

In contrast, think of the wise *man of dominion* who for years pushed himself to overcome his passive lethargy. After dinner, he faithfully taught his daughter from the Bible. In the evening, he climbed out of his sofa in order to tuck her into bed. In the dead of night, when she cried out in fear, he rushed to her aid; when she vomited all over the sheets, he was there to clean it up. When she went through a phase of lying, he was there with consistent discipline to break her of the sin. When she wanted to talk past her bedtime, he was there to listen and laugh.

When that kind of a father has to say to his daughter, "Honey, I know that you like him, but your mother and I are convinced it wouldn't be a good thing. He could never spiritually lead you. You know that your daddy only wants the best for you, don't you?" That father is well positioned to hear, though through a mist of tears, "I know, but it just hurts so much, daddy!"

That same daddy is also well positioned to say such things as:

> "Honey, have him give me a call and we'll discuss his coming over to meet your mother and me."
>
> "Honey, we think it would be best if you only saw him once per month for now."

"Yes, it would be my privilege to give you my daughter's hand in marriage."

"A toast to my new son-in-law, a true man after God's own heart!"

In conclusion, a Christian parent, exercising *manly dominion*, will not passively sit back and watch his offspring naively wander into the American "dating game." Just because we're in Canaan, we need not conform to the Canaanites.

Fathers, we need to step up, and *subdue* and *rule* in relationship overseeing. And I assure you, this is more easily said than done. Such a conviction will need to be practically pursued by careful instructions, courageous confrontations, prayerful supplications, and long late-night conversations with emotionally-charged young people. It's not a mission for a faint-of-heart *passive-purple-four-ball*.

It requires *manly dominion*.

31 / FATHERLY OVERSEEING OF RELATIONSHIPS

1 *The Christian Father's Present to His Children*, p.368
2 Derek Kidner, *Proverbs* (Downer's Grove, IL: InterVarsity Press, 1964), p.156
3 op. cit., p.146

About the Author

Mark Chanski has labored as a full-time Pastor since 1986 in churches in Ohio and Michigan. He has been Pastor of the Reformed Baptist Church of Holland, Michigan since 1994. He holds a Bachelor's degree from Cornerstone University, and a Master of Divinity degree from Grand Rapids Baptist Seminary. Mark is married to his wife Dianne, and fathers their four sons and one daughter, whose ages stretch from 10 to 20.